THE CITY & GUILDS

PRACTICAL GUIDE TO QUALITY ASSURANCE

KAREN PONTIN

City&
Guilds

About City & Guilds

City & Guilds is the UK's leading provider of vocational qualifications, offering over 500 awards across a wide range of industries, and progressing from entry level to the highest levels of professional achievement. With over 8500 centres in 100 countries, City & Guilds is recognised by employers worldwide for providing qualifications that offer proof of the skills they need to get the job done.

Equal opportunities

City & Guilds fully supports the principle of equal opportunities and we are committed to satisfying this principle in all our activities and published material. A copy of our equal opportunities policy statement is available on the City & Guilds website.

Copyright

The content of this document is, unless otherwise indicated, © The City and Guilds of London Institute 2012 and may not be copied, reproduced or distributed without prior written consent.

First edition 2012

ISBN 978 0 85193 238 5

Cover design by Select Typesetters Ltd
Typeset by Integra Software Services Pvt. Ltd
Printed in the UK by CLOC

Publications

For information about or to order City & Guilds support materials, contact 0844 534 0000 or centresupport@cityandguilds.com. You can find more information about the materials we have available at www.cityandguilds.com/publications.

Every effort has been made to ensure that the information contained in this publication is true and correct at the time of going to press. However, City & Guilds' products and services are subject to continuous development and improvement and the right is reserved to change products and services from time to time. City & Guilds cannot accept liability for loss or damage arising from the use of information in this publication.

City & Guilds
1 Giltspur Street
London EC1A 9DD

T 0844 543 0033
www.cityandguilds.com
publishingfeedback@cityandguilds.com

CONTENTS

ACKNOWLEDGEMENTS

Sincere thanks to the people who personally or by their work have supported me in producing this book. Special thanks to Melissa Woods and Charmain Campbell, without whom it would not have happened at all. Also to colleagues at City & Guilds and Neath Port Talbot County Borough Council Lifelong Learning Service for allowing me to reproduce some of their materials, the City & Guilds publishing team for their encouragement, Rachel Blake and Linda Orr for reviewing the manuscript, and my family, whose long-suffering forbearance I have surely exhausted.

City & Guilds would like to thank the following organisations for giving permission to reproduce their materials:

Joanna Hurren for the 'What is an IQA 'sample?' ' explanation in Part 2.

Phil Southard at Neath Port Talbot County Borough Council Lifelong Learning service for the internal quality assurance example strategy documents in Appendix 4.

Picture credits

Every effort has been made to acknowledge all copyright holders as below and publishers will, if notified, correct any errors in future editions.

Shutterstock: 11, 12, 15, 19, 20, 21, 29, 31, 32, 33, 35, 37, 40, 41, 61, 62, 66, 71, 74, 76, 82, 86, 87, 90, 93, 96, 97, 101, 102, 104, 107, 109, 111, 115, 117, 118, 121, 123, 126, 128, 130, 131, 133, 141, 144,146, 149, 151, 153, 154, 155, 157, 159, 161, 163, 164, 165, 170, 171, 172, 174, 175, 177, 181, 183.

ABOUT THE AUTHOR

Karen Pontin is an experienced Internal Quality Assurer (IQA) and External Quality Assurer (EQA) who has worked for 30 years as an adviser in the fields of Management, and Learning and Development. She is a Standardisation Consultant for City & Guilds in Wales and supports a team of 15 other EQAs in that role. In addition she is a Systems Consultant and the national adviser for Learning and Development qualifications (which include the qualifications for Assessment, Internal and External Quality Assurance) to the City & Guilds Portfolio Team, who manage all Learning qualifications. She was involved in the development of the 2010 Assessment and Quality Assurance qualifications and was one of the team who wrote the Qualification Handbook to support them. She acts as the technical adviser on Assessment and Quality Assurance qualifications on City & Guilds SmartScreen. Karen has been involved in the world of training and development since leaving teaching in 1982. She lives in Swansea with her family and has been self-employed since 1988.

INTRODUCTION

In general terms, quality assurance is a system of monitoring and checking the quality of a product or service to ensure that it consistently meets the specified standards.

It has been used for decades in a range of fields as a way of maintaining and improving services and products.

Although quality assurance *in learning* works on the same principles, it is not primarily about auditing, sampling and ticking boxes. It is about a system for maintaining and improving standards on an ongoing basis.

This system requires knowledgeable people, a strategy, plans, procedures, reporting, checks and balances to ensure that everything goes smoothly, requirements are met and any issues are identified and remedied quickly so that learners have a positive experience and achieve their goals.

If you are employed in a quality assurance role in a learning organisation, work on qualifications that are quality assured, if you are a learner in quality assurance or just interested in what quality assurance in learning means, then this book will be of interest to you.

By reading this book, you will come to understand how quality assurance is fundamental to the entire process of delivering learning – from recruitment onto a programme, through to the achievement of a level of ability or a qualification. You will also become aware of its role in all stages of the learning cycle, including:

- planning and preparation
- resourcing
- learning delivery and facilitating learning
- assessment
- record keeping
- evaluation.

This book has come about as a result of my experiences in internal and external quality assurance, where I recognised that there is very little source material for people new to the field. This is not meant to be an academic tome, nor, sadly, can it provide all the answers, but it does aim to be a practical handbook that will give practitioners useful insights into what quality assurance is in the context of 'learning' and why it is so important, and provide some practical tools that may help to improve quality assurance practice – whether it is being done on an internal or external basis.

Although there are similarities between internal and external quality assurance, for ease of reference the book is separated into three parts: Part 1 focuses on an overview of quality assurance, Part 2 on internal quality assurance and Part 3 on external quality assurance.

You may want to read Parts One and Two or Parts One and Three depending upon your role and interest. However, you may find that reading all three will help you to make sense of quality assurance both inside a centre and in the context of the 'bigger picture'.

This book is compatible with the National Occupational Standards (NOS) for Learning and Development, NOS Standard 11 for Internal Quality Assurance and NOS Standard 12 for External Quality Assurance (LLUK March 2010).

It will also support learners undertaking the following City & Guilds qualifications:

- 6317 - Internal Quality Assurance qualifications
- 6312 - External Quality Assurance qualifications

6317 Internal Quality Assurance
Level 4 Award in Understanding the Internal Quality Assurance of Assessment Processes and Practice

Level 4 Award in the Internal Quality Assurance of Assessment Processes and Practice

Where the text relates directly to an Assessment Criteria (AC) in the 6317 unit you will find it referenced in this manner: [6317 Unit 401 AC 1.1]

6312 External Quality Assurance
Level 4 Award in Understanding the External Quality Assurance of Assessment Processes and Practice

Level 4 Award in the External Quality Assurance of Assessment Processes and Practice

Where the text relates directly to an Assessment Criteria (AC) in the 6312 unit you will find it referenced in this manner: [6312 Unit 404 AC 1.1]

The terminology and information in this book are correct at time of writing.

The following table gives an overview of the roles and responsibilities of everyone who is likely to be involved in internal quality assurance [6317 unit 401 AC 1.3]:

Role	Description	Typical responsibilities
Quality Manager	Usually a member of the centre's senior management team. May not hold tutor, assessment or Internal Quality Assurer (IQA) qualifications.	The Quality Manager: • generally does not carry out any IQA duties • has little operational involvement • drives forward improvements in a centre's quality • sets policy on quality and related issues • is responsible for internal communication on quality issues • ensures quality has a high profile in the senior management team • organises the external inspections that take place • manages quality initiatives • line manages the Quality Assurance Co-ordinator (QAC) or IQA Co-ordinator (IQAC) • seeks to ensure consistency and promote best practice across departments/sectors.
Quality Assurance Co-ordinator (QAC) or Centre Contact	Operational manager of the internal quality assurance function. Often carries out some IQA duties. Manages entire centre or one department. Some organisations have a lead or senior IQA for this role.	The QAC usually plans the following on an annual basis: • intakes of learners • team meetings • internal audits • self-assessments for external agencies • standardisation between IQAs • observations of IQAs • line management of the IQAs • external quality assurance visits/remote sampling.
Internal Quality Assurer (IQA)	Usually assigned to a small number of programmes and/or qualifications. Have previously been tutors and/or assessors for these programmes. They have a detailed understanding of programme or qualification requirements.	The main responsibilities are usually to: • maintain the integrity of the programme or qualification being delivered • lead improvements in the learning delivery • ensure assessors interpret, understand and apply the standards and requirements their learners are working towards • plan and carry out sampling of assessed work using CAMERA (see page 41). • monitor delivery and assessment practice • interview learners and witnesses • document the quality assurance process and decisions • identify issues and trends • observe tutors and assessors working with learners • provide feedback to tutors and assessors • advise and support tutors and assessors • lead standardisation activities to ensure accuracy and consistency of assessment decisions between assessors • take part in Continuing Professional Development (CPD).

Role	Description	Typical responsibilities
IQA *continued*		IQAs are also sometimes required to: • chair meetings • countersign other quality assurers' judgements • deal with any assessment appeals and complaints • manage grievances raised against members of the team • liaise with others involved in the IQA process, eg External Quality Assurers (EQAs) • implement external quality assurance action points • provide statistics and reports to line managers • carry out training needs analysis with tutors and assessors.
Tutor	Person who delivers or facilitates the learning that takes place on any programme. May deliver to groups of learners or carry out one-to-one coaching. Sometimes the same person as the assessor on the programme.	The main responsibilities of the tutor are usually to: • engage learners in the programme • plan, prepare or source materials • carry out induction into the qualification • identify learning needs • manage the learners • plan the learning delivery • deliver the material • monitor learner engagement and progress • evaluate the programme • take part in CPD.
Assessor	A subject or topic expert who holds the experience, knowledge and skills as required in the assessment strategy to assess any particular programme or qualification. They have to be named as responsible for the assessment decisions that they take and accept that their work is subject to internal and external quality assurance.	The main responsibilities of an assessor would usually be to: • understand and apply the standards and requirements if learners are working towards qualifications • plan assessments to meet learner needs • communicate assessment requirements to learners • carry out assessments • compare evidence with set standards/criteria • make assessment decisions • document the assessment process and decisions • provide feedback to learners • take part in standardisation processes • take part in CPD.

Role	Description	Typical responsibilities
		They might also be required to: • attend meetings • check the authenticity of witness testimonies • countersign other assessors' judgements • identify and overcome (if possible) any barriers to fair assessment • implement internal and external quality assurance action points • justify their decisions, ie if an appeal is made against them • liaise with others involved in the assessment process • provide information to IQAs or managers • review learner progress • produce reports for IQAs, supervisors or employers.

ACTIVITY

To start your thinking about the process, first consider your role. Whichever of the above roles you carry out, how many of the activities listed are you responsible for? Who carried out the others in the list?

PART 1:
OVERVIEW OF QUALITY ASSURANCE IN LEARNING

What does quality assurance in learning entail, and what is its place in a national or regulatory context?

SO WHAT EXACTLY IS QUALITY ASSURANCE IN LEARNING?

It is a system that ensures that someone plans and prepares how the quality assurance programme will be structured, when it will be monitored and that the resources for monitoring are in place. Every feature of the delivery of learning will be monitored, including planning, actual delivery, assessment, reviewing and record keeping. Improvements are then introduced as the programme moves forward.

As the process progresses, planned reviews and evaluations are carried out and further improvements introduced. These actions may be undertaken by one or more individuals according to the size and structure of an organisation.

In a college spread over six sites there may be one Quality Manager, three Lead Quality Assurers and 35 IQAs. They will all have a different role to play, but between them they will cover every part of the 'learner journey'. In a small training centre with six assessors and only one IQA, that person may be solely responsible for ensuring the quality of the entire learner experience. These various models are discussed in later sections.

WHY QUALITY ASSURE?

If only it were possible to set up an activity or process in the sure knowledge that it would all be run well, meet the requirements and achieve its targets. Unfortunately this rarely happens without someone drafting out plans, agreeing who does what and checking that planned actions have taken place, that nothing unforeseen has arisen and that targets or deadlines are being met. In the majority of cases anything left to chance either does not happen at all or goes badly wrong. Quality assurance in its broadest sense is a way of building processes that set up objectives then check that the required actions are planned, carried out and achieved.

Inevitably, to achieve progress someone has to own and manage the processes involved. In many organisations the role of IQA falls to the manager of a process because in many respects quality assurance and management processes are very similar. Both roles require the person to plan, gain the co-operation of other people, allocate and monitor other people's work and give feedback to those people on their performance. In both roles the person has to take responsibility for the activity being completed and meeting the requirements.

Ultimately, both are responsible for the quality of what takes place. Quality assurance is a system or series of processes for making this happen.

Good quality assurance gives a measure of control over activities and can provide tangible benefits for everyone involved in the process of delivering learning. Benefits include:

For organisations – if programmes are well organised, run to plan, and then regularly reviewed and improved, this should lead to:
- improved learner experience
- raised learner achievement rates
- increased learner retention rates
- more cost-effective programmes
- regulatory requirements being met
- support for other planning and monitoring processes, such as self-assessment.

For the person embarking on the learning – quality assurance impacts on their experiences at every stage of their 'learner journey' and should improve their:
- pre-programme experience
- induction
- initial assessment
- learning plans
- learning experience
- reviews of progress
- assessment
- achievement
- progression planning.

For those delivering the programme – quality assurance gives:
- clear direction
- guidance on what is expected of them
- support on a planned basis
- feedback
- a reporting structure.

Total Quality Management (TQM) sums up quality as 'Getting it right – first time and every time.'

As a result, everyone should have confidence in the process and its outcomes when someone ensures the quality of the inputs. In learning, this means ensuring that the people, the content and the structure being delivered have been planned, monitored and evaluated.

Whoever is doing each part of the process, the following will all need to be covered. Someone will:

- ensure the programme is run in a 'fit and proper' manner
- ensure quality in the planning process
- assess and manage risk
- monitor the quality of training delivery, coaching, assessment and reviewing

- identify issues and trends
- ensure team members comply with the assessment strategy for the qualification they are working with (if applicable)
- ensure the accuracy and consistency of assessment decisions between assessors
- ensure that team members are consistent in their interpretation of the criteria that they are involved in delivering
- identify the development needs of all team members
- create development opportunities for all team members
- support and ensure the Continuing Professional Development (CPD) of all team members.

As mentioned above, in order to achieve its aims the process requires effective systems, sustained attention and committed professional people. In addition these need to work smoothly together and interact to result in effective quality assurance. The process needs to look something like this:

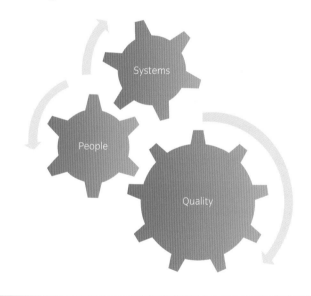

Achieving quality requires time and effort from everyone involved, plus good planning and ongoing monitoring. It's a circular process – not a one-off activity – and needs to be part of the overall commitment to providing a quality service to learners.

ACTIVITY

Consider for a moment the simplified model above. Of the three 'cogs', which do you think might be most likely to cause the model to grind to a halt?

However important it is that everyone involved in delivering learning is committed to 'getting things right', there are also national, regulatory and in some cases statutory requirements for quality assurance in the UK, which permeate down to requirements within individual organisations delivering the learning.

When an organisation decides to deliver an accredited qualification or any externally validated programme of learning, they will have to meet a series of requirements from their Awarding Organisation (AO) in order to be 'approved' to deliver that programme or qualification (eg City & Guilds). This is where quality assurance on recognised qualifications begins – meeting the criteria set by the AO is the first step in ensuring quality.

For an example of the criteria set by an AO, go to www.cityandguilds.com, and look at the online documents for assisting organisations to become 'approved centres'. Most other AOs will also have something similar.

Once the organisation has become an 'approved centre' and is able to deliver one or more qualifications, then the AO has to ensure that the arrangements continue to meet the requirements over time and as situations, the organisation – and in particular staffing – change. The monitoring that the AOs put in place to confirm that the requirements are met is the essence of external quality assurance (see Part 3), whereas the internal self-monitoring that AOs require of approved centres is known as internal quality assurance (see Part 2).

THE NATIONAL PICTURE

SECTOR SKILLS COUNCILS AND STANDARDS SETTING BODIES

There are a range of external bodies that represent employer interests and the interests of their occupational sector, and these may have a role in determining what quality assurance measures have to be in place. These are currently called Sector Skills Councils (SSCs) or Standards Setting Bodies (SSBs). They consult with stakeholders (in particular, employers and AOs) to determine whether there is a need for an accredited programme or qualification for that specific sector. If the need does exist, they then work with interested parties to develop programmes and qualifications, plus the assessment guidance or strategies that outline how the qualification must be delivered. For a list of SSCs and to identify which ones cover the occupational area in which you work or are interested, see: www.ukces.org.uk/sector-skills-councils/about-sscs/the-list-of-sscs/

NATIONAL REGULATORS FOR QUALIFICATIONS AND ASSESSMENT

In addition to requirements set by the SSC for the delivery of an accredited programme or qualification, there are also other external quality assurance requirements set by national regulators for any 'regulated' qualifications.

The regulators are primarily responsible for ensuring that the AOs themselves meet quality requirements for managing qualifications. Inevitably these requirements distil down to become requirements of the individual organisations who deliver the learning. The regulators are currently as follows:

- Ofqual in England: www.ofqual.gov.uk
- CCEA in Northern Ireland: www.rewardinglearning.org.uk
- DfES in Wales: http://wales.gov.uk/topics/educationandskills/ qualificationsinwales
- SQA in Scotland: www.sqa.org.uk

ACTIVITY [6317 unit 401 AC1.4]

Visit the website of the SSC/SSBs and the regulator related to your occupational area and country. What quality assurance measures do they use? How does this affect or impact on the learning that you are involved in?

As an *aide memoire*, think of the levels of quality assurance in the UK as an onion – the qualification or learning programme is in the middle, the next layer moving towards the outside is the *internal* quality assurance, the next layer is the *external* quality assurance, then the AO, then the SSC and finally the regulators.

Each of these layers is involved in the work of the one beneath, so the regulators oversee the AOs, the AO representative – the EQA – monitors the approved centres who deliver the qualifications and programmes, and the IQA oversees what goes on inside the centre that is actually delivering the learning.

There are also inspection agencies that have a role in quality assurance of the delivery of qualifications – ie the 'inputs' to the qualifications. These are listed in the table below.

Agency	Country	Purpose
OFSTED www.ofsted.gov.uk *'Ofsted is the Office for Standards in Education, Children's Services and Skills'*	England	'We inspect and regulate services which care for children and young people, and those providing education and skills for learners of all ages.'
ETI www.etini.gov.uk *'ETI is part of the Department for Education of the Northern Ireland Assembly'*	Northern Ireland	'The purpose of inspection is to promote the highest possible standards of learning, teaching and achievement throughout the education, training and youth sectors.'
ESTYN www.estyn.gov.uk *'Estyn is the office of Her Majesty's Inspectorate for Education and Training in Wales. We are independent of, but funded by, the National Assembly for Wales'*	Wales	'The purpose of Estyn is to inspect quality and standards in education and training in Wales.'
Education Scotland www.educationscotland.gov.uk *'Education Scotland has been established by the Scottish Government Cabinet Secretary for Education and Lifelong Learning as a key national body supporting quality and improvement in Scottish education'*	Scotland	'The purpose and aims of the inspection process in evaluating the quality of learning and teaching in Scottish schools and education services.'

ACTIVITY

Look at the website of the inspection agency for the country where you primarily work. Does it have the same aims as the regulators? How would you summarise the main differences in the remit of the regulators and the inspectors in your country?

The national 'quality assurance in learning' picture looks something like this:

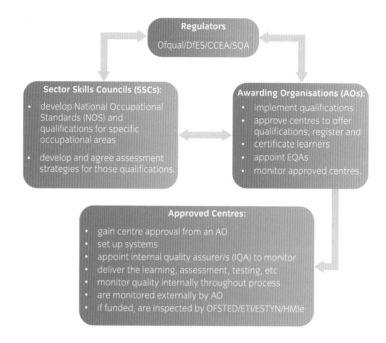

HOW IS THE NATIONAL PICTURE IMPLEMENTED LOCALLY?

Keep up to date with the terminology used by your AO by signing up on their website for updates.

As described above, the national requirements set by the SSC/SSB and regulators are interpreted by the AOs. They use and implement agreed criteria for approving centres, and as part of this process they put in place a system of external quality assurance (see Part 3). They in turn require that the approved centres introduce their own quality assurance system called (understandably) internal quality assurance (see Part 2). Therefore on a local basis the model is fairly simple and looks something like this:

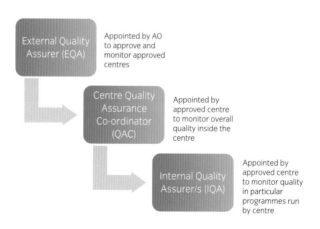

WHY IS NATIONAL QUALITY ASSURANCE IMPORTANT? [6317 unit 401 AC1.1]

It is in everyone's interest for the delivery of accredited programmes and qualifications in the UK to be of the highest quality. In order for everyone to have confidence in the outcomes of the learning (eg qualifications), the system used to develop and ensure this quality has to be – and be seen to be – robust and of the highest integrity.

After all, accredited programmes or nationally recognised qualifications are some of the measures that everyone – and in particular employers – use to determine a person's skills, ability and knowledge. If a person has a qualification, this will very often assist an employer to make the decision as to whether an applicant for a job can perform a role. Working towards a qualification may also form part of the ongoing training and development achievement that employers expect of their staff.

For an individual, the programme or qualification is one of the factors that will help them to secure employment, and may play an ongoing part in ensuring that they can provide for themselves and others.

From the standpoint of business in the UK, people completing accredited programmes and achieving qualifications is a vital measure of their commitment, skills, knowledge and ability. It also assists in ensuring that required skills are available to develop products and services that meet market needs, and so drive the economy and enable the UK to compete across the globe.

Therefore it is vital that all parties have confidence in the accreditation and qualification system, and the processes that check, monitor and evaluate that system. If the quality assurance system was not effective in maintaining and improving the quality of qualifications, this confidence would quickly evaporate.

ACTIVITY

You have had your car serviced and repaired at the same garage for five years and the service has always been very good. The managing mechanic was trained on the make of vehicle that you drive, has a great deal of experience, is fully qualified and is knowledgeable.

An indicator light on the dashboard is showing that the brake pads on your car need to be replaced and in addition the brakes need adjustment.

When you take the car in to the garage the manager says that JT will look after your car from now on. He left college early so he's not qualified – but he's a 'good lad' and a fast learner.

How would you react?

If you were not confident that the person repairing the brakes on your car had been fully trained and carefully assessed, would you be convinced of their skills and abilities? How had they been measured? How would that make you feel?

Whenever you are relying on someone, you want to feel secure that they are qualified. This security also comes from feeling sure that when they did qualify they really had 'made the grade'. In order to have this confidence we all need to know that there are robust checks and assessment in the learning process to ensure that that person's skills and knowledge are complete and current, and that their performance has been thoroughly tested. This is what quality assurance in learning seeks to guarantee.

It is for exactly these sorts of reasons that a national quality assurance system exists. It enables everyone – learners, employers, government and the public – to have confidence that when someone completes an accredited programme or achieves a qualification they have the skills, knowledge and ability to carry out those tasks to an agreed industry standard.

It ensures that:
- the integrity of qualifications is maintained
- public confidence in qualifications is protected
- there is a level of regulatory control over how qualifications are achieved
- there is a measure of consistency in the content of qualifications
- assessment decisions are consistent.

If qualifications are not credible, we risk undermining our system of measuring skills, abilities and knowledge.

In summary, the national quality assurance system exists to establish and monitor the processes that will ensure that standards are met, and it seeks to instil confidence and develop excellence.

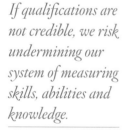

SUMMARY

The following points were covered in Part 1: Overview of quality assurance in learning:
- what constitutes quality assurance in learning
- why quality assurance is carried out
- the national picture
- why national quality assurance is so important.

PART 2: INTERNAL QUALITY ASSURANCE

What are the roles and functions involved in internal quality assurance in learning? Among other things, how should you tackle the planning process, sampling work and maintaining records?

MODELS OF INTERNAL QUALITY ASSURANCE

As described in Part 1, the national requirements for quality assurance are managed in a hierarchy, from the regulators, through to the AOs, down to delivery on a local basis in individual approved centres.

'Quality is the degree of excellence of something' (Concise Oxford Dictionary 8ᵗʰ Ed)

'Quality assurance is a system of maintaining and improving standards'

Each AO manages the external quality assurance process differently, and indeed each centre may organise its internal procedures in a way that best suits it. This has resulted in a number of similar but different models being developed for how centres manage internal quality assurance. These might vary from one person acting as IQA and organising everything in a small centre delivering only a limited number of qualifications, through to up to 50 people being involved in the process in large multi-sector organisations.

In addition, different organisations use different terminology, so a role called Lead IQA in one organisation may be called Senior IQA in another. The role called QAC in one organisation may be termed IQA Co-ordinator (IQAC) in another. Also, people may carry out more than one role in a centre – so they might be both IQA and QAC in a small centre, whereas these roles would be carried out by two or more people in a larger centre.

Below are some of the most common models currently in use.

This model is fairly typical of a centre with a small number of tutors/assessors:

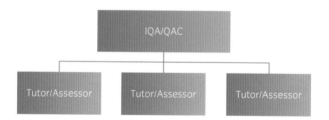

The tutor/assessors would be working on one or more qualifications about which the IQA is likely to be very knowledgeable. The IQA may also carry out the role of the QAC (described further in the next section) – they are likely to take responsibility for managing the learning delivery and assessment processes and liaison with the AO. In this model, the IQA may also be the manager of the team, head of the section or department and even the owner/manager of the organisation.

This would be the model most often seen in a medium-sized centre:

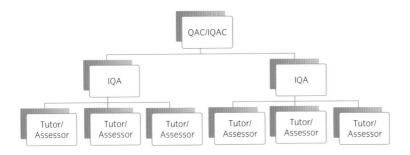

In a centre using this model there would generally be a number of qualifications being delivered, with assessors reporting to an IQA who is likely to be knowledgeable about the qualifications. The IQAs in turn report to the QAC or IQAC, who is likely to be less expert in the individual qualifications but may be knowledgeable in the sector. However, even though they may still carry out IQA duties, they would primarily have a managerial role.

In a more complex centre, inevitably the internal quality assurance model is more complex:

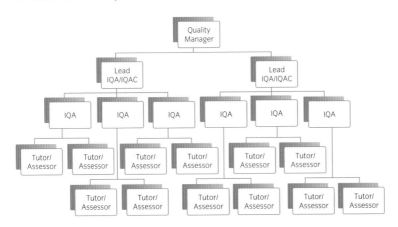

Centres using this model generally deliver a large number of qualifications with teams of tutors and assessors reporting to an IQA, who is likely to be knowledgeable about the qualifications the team members deliver.

These IQAs in turn report to a Lead IQA or IQAC, who would be likely to be an experienced IQA who is now in a role co-ordinating the work of other IQAs – and who oversees a number of qualifications. The Lead IQA/IQACs sometimes act in a similar role to that of the QAC in smaller centres. Lead IQA/IQACs often report to a Quality Manager who may be a 'quality' expert with little or no knowledge of the individual qualifications being delivered.

The Quality Manager might also be carrying out the role of overall QAC or Centre Contact, but they would primarily manage the Lead IQA/IQACs and may be responsible for a number of departments, sections and different types of qualifications.

These are the most common models that centres use to organise their internal quality assurance, but there are others – specific to individual organisations – that will have evolved as a centre has grown.

ACTIVITY

If you are familiar with a centre, think about/find out about their internal quality assurance. What model do they use? Why do they use that particular structure?

There are a number of roles involved in a quality assurance system (see page 29 for details).The role and function of internal quality assurance is generally as follows [6317 unit 401 AC 1.1].

As described previously, AOs make sure that quality assurance continues from external factors into internal systems by requiring all providers of their learning programmes and/or qualifications to operate their own internal quality assurance systems. These systems vary between AOs, but fundamentally they aim to achieve the same goal – to ensure that all learning delivery and assessment is of a high standard.

Inevitably different AOs use different models of external quality assurance, depending on the type and nature of the qualifications being delivered. For example, quality assuring a centre that is delivering a qualification taught on a timetabled number of hours in one site (such as an A level delivered in a college), assessed by an end 'exam' that is set and marked by the AO itself, requires a particular model. Alternatively, a training centre where learning primarily takes place on an employer's premises, assessment is carried out whenever the learner is ready and the main assessment method is observation, demands a different and perhaps more complex model.

Similarly, internal quality assurance systems can differ hugely in the way they are organised and run, depending on the nature of the centre itself, the qualifications being delivered and the culture of that particular organisation.

As outlined in the previous section, in large organisations there may be more than one person responsible for the quality assurance activities carried out – there may even be a dedicated internal quality team. However, in smaller, flatter organisations one person may carry out all these roles.

Whichever model is used, and however it is organised, everyone involved in 'quality' will have the same overall aims in mind – to ensure the following:

- arrangements for delivering the programme or qualification meet the requirements
- the right people are involved in the delivery
- the best possible resources are available for the learning and assessment
- suitable checks and balances are in place to monitor the delivery throughout
- a good experience for the learner
- high retention and achievement rates.

Unfortunately, as with most quality products and services, none of it happens by chance. To achieve the above, it is necessary for someone to take responsibility for making sure that:

- there are procedures in place outlining how things should be done
- appropriate planning takes place
- learning delivery is monitored
- assessment decisions taken are standardised and reliable across assessors
- tutors and/or assessors have the support and development that they need
- records of all learning, assessment and internal quality assurance are accurate, kept up to date, sufficiently detailed and complete.

The role of quality assurance inside a learning organisation is fundamental to ensuring quality in the delivery of learning. It is how a centre manages the learner's experience while following a qualification or learning programme. It is the fundamental system for ensuring that the experience is positive and everything that is put in place is designed to meet the specified target outcomes.

In summary, internal quality assurance in learning is a system of agreeing what is needed, securing resources, building the programme and then checking to see that what is actually happening continues to meet the original agreed outcomes.

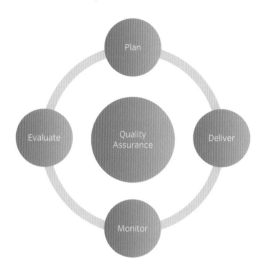

Everything else in internal quality assurance is simply about ensuring that this cycle takes place.

ACTIVITY [6317 unit 401 AC 1.1]

From what you have read so far, what actions do you think IQAs carry out? What are the main functions needed for successful internal quality assurance? Why is it so important?

THE MAIN FUNCTIONS OF INTERNAL QUALITY ASSURANCE

Internal quality assurance is meant to ensure that a range of functions are carried out. You may have identified some of main ones, which are listed in the table below.

Internal quality assurance function	What it entails
Assessing and managing risk	The amount, methods and type of quality assurance that takes place is dependent on the assessment of risk in the qualifications being delivered. Risk may be caused by a variety of factors, such as new requirements in the qualifications, new staff, known problem modules, etc.
Communication	Internal quality assurance is meant to ensure that information about national requirements and issues are passed from the 'macro' (eg from the AOs) to the 'micro' (inside the centre).

Internal quality assurance function	What it entails
Compliance	This entails checking that the requirements of the regulators, the awarding organisations, inspectors, the organisation and the delivery of the qualification itself are met.
Ensuring accuracy and consistency	This means taking action before, during and at the conclusion of learning delivery, to make sure that all learning (ie inputs) delivered, and assessment decisions (ie outcomes) taken, are accurate and similar – irrespective of who is involved.
Identifying issues and trends	The IQA is in the most appropriate position to identify where recurring issues happen (such as problems with one particular unit) and to be able to identify trends in assessment practice (such as inaccurate marking of assignments in a particular module).
Planning	The IQA will ensure that all aspects of the learner experience and the delivery of the programme or qualification are planned, but also that the quality assurance process itself is based on a sound rationale, is planned and is neither random nor ad hoc.
Record keeping	It is important that detailed and complete records of actions planned and carried out are maintained – and that these records are kept in line with the requirements of the AO.
Resourcing	This means guaranteeing that the necessary resources – human, physical or financial – are available to meet the requirements of the programme/qualification.
Sampling	The IQA will look at a representative sample of the work of others to ensure that it meets the requirements of the regulators, the AOs, inspectors, the organisation and the specifics of the qualification itself.
Supporting and developing assessors	This is the main mechanism that IQAs use to effect improvement in assessment practice and so is a very important function.
Taking decisions	In a whole range of areas – these might include decisions about the suitability of staff to deliver the qualifications, through to deciding whether to finally confirm the assessment decisions and so 'sign off' a learner's work.
Upholding integrity	Another major function of IQA was termed in the past 'guarding the standards' – in other words, making sure that whatever pressures the IQA or assessors are put under, the quality of the delivery of the programme or qualifications is not compromised and all requirements continue to be met.

Store your IQA data electronically wherever possible.

An internal quality assurance tale...

There was a centre that had been delivering qualifications for a few years but whose internal quality assurance records were sketchy. Minutes of meetings tended to be one line per agenda item and there was little proof that standardisation of assessment practice really took place. The EQA gave the centre relevant action points on a number of occasions in an attempt to guide them to improve the detail of what and how they recorded the work carried out, but there was little improvement. The EQA was sufficiently concerned about the lack of progress in the recording of internal quality assurance at the centre that he insisted on observing a meeting where standardisation was to take place.

He duly observed the meeting and was very pleased to see that real standardisation did take place, with assessors looking at each other's work and comparing assessment decisions. He again instructed the centre to keep detailed records of that activity and all others.

The moral of the story is that in order to do internal quality assurance practice justice, centres need to keep sufficiently detailed records of what they do. Doing it is not sufficient – IQAs need to be able to prove that they do it! Improving record keeping may also contribute to the AO reducing the number of external quality assurance visits the centre has in any year.

These functions can be grouped into four main and complementary areas of IQA practice:

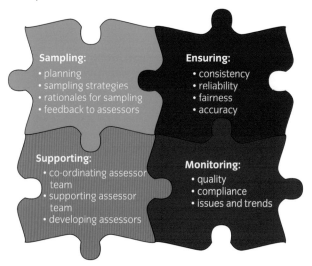

Sampling:
• planning
• sampling strategies
• rationales for sampling
• feedback to assessors

Ensuring:
• consistency
• reliability
• fairness
• accuracy

Supporting:
• co-ordinating assessor team
• supporting assessor team
• developing assessors

Monitoring:
• quality
• compliance
• issues and trends

If you are already an IQA, check to see if your job description or role profile includes all of these areas.

Each of these areas of practice relies on the others, and together they make up the full IQA role.

ROLES AND RESPONSIBILITIES IN THE INTERNAL QUALITY ASSURANCE TEAM

[6317 unit 401 AC 1.3]

As you saw in the Introduction (see page 8), there are a number of possible roles required by the IQA process, depending on which model the centre is using. Here is more information on each of them.

QUALITY MANAGER

The Quality Manager is usually a member of the senior management team in the centre and generally does not carry out any internal quality assurance duties. In many centres they have little operational involvement, but they are responsible for driving forward improvements in quality. They may hold no tutor, assessment or IQA qualifications and have little experience of carrying out any of the functions. In some cases they have never been involved in learning delivery before, but have experience of quality assurance in another capacity, eg in relation to a product.

They may be the person who:
- sets policy on quality and related issues
- is responsible for internal communication on quality issues
- ensures quality has a high profile in the senior management team
- organises the external inspections that take place
- manages quality initiatives
- line manages the QAC or IQACs
- seeks to ensure consistency and promote best practice across departments/sectors.

QUALITY ASSURANCE CO-ORDINATOR (QAC) OR CENTRE CONTACT

The QAC tends to be the operational manager of the internal quality assurance function, and will often still carry out some IQA duties themselves. They may manage the entire centre or be responsible for only one department. In some organisations these responsibilities may be carried out by a Lead or Senior IQA.

On an annual basis, they are likely to be the person who plans out:
- intakes of learners
- team meetings
- internal audits
- self-assessments for external agencies
- standardisation between IQAs
- observations of IQAs
- line management of the IQAs
- external quality assurance visits/remote sampling.

INTERNAL QUALITY ASSURER (IQA)

The IQA is usually assigned to a small number of programmes and/ or qualifications. They have often previously been tutors and/or assessors of these same programmes or qualifications and have a detailed understanding of how they operate and the requirements they contain. Their experience is a vital component in their ability to guide and support tutors and assessors to improve their practice.

The main responsibilities of an IQA would usually be to:
- maintain the integrity of the programme or qualification being delivered
- lead improvements in the learning delivery
- ensure assessors interpret, understand and apply the standards and requirements their learners are working towards
- plan and carry out sampling of assessed work using CAMERA (see page 41)
- monitor delivery and assessment practice
- interview learners and witnesses
- document the quality assurance process and decisions
- identify issues and trends
- observe tutors and assessors working with learners
- provide feedback to tutors and assessors
- advise and support tutors and assessors
- lead standardisation activities to ensure accuracy and consistency of assessment decisions between assessors
- take part in CPD.

IQAs are also sometimes required to:
- chair meetings
- countersign other quality assurers' judgements
- deal with any assessment appeals and complaints
- manage grievances raised against members of the team
- liaise with others involved in the internal quality assurance process, eg EQAs
- implement external quality assurance action points
- provide statistics and reports to line managers
- carry out training needs analysis with tutors and assessors.

TUTOR

The tutor is the person who delivers or facilitates the learning that takes place on any programme. They may deliver to groups of learners or by working one-to-one in more of a coaching role. They are sometimes the same person as the assessor on the programme – on other programmes the roles are carried out by different people.

The main responsibilities of the tutor are usually to:

- engage learners in the programme
- plan, prepare or source materials
- carry out induction into the qualification
- identify learning needs
- manage the learners
- plan the learning delivery
- deliver the material
- monitor learner engagement and progress
- evaluate the programme
- take part in CPD.

ASSESSOR

The assessor is a subject or topic expert who holds the experience, knowledge and skills as required in the assessment strategy to assess any particular programme or qualification. They have to be named as responsible for the assessment decisions that they take and accept that their work is subject to internal and external quality assurance.

The main responsibilities of an assessor would usually be to:

- understand and apply the standards and requirements if learners are working towards qualifications
- plan assessments to meet learner needs
- communicate assessment requirements to learners
- carry out assessments
- compare evidence with set standards/criteria
- make assessment decisions
- document the assessment process and decisions
- provide feedback to learners
- take part in standardisation processes
- take part in CPD.

They might also be required to:

- attend meetings
- check the authenticity of witness testimonies
- countersign other assessors' judgements
- identify and overcome (if possible) any barriers to fair assessment
- implement internal and external quality assurance action points
- justify their decisions, ie if an appeal is made against them
- liaise with others involved in the assessment process
- provide information to IQAs or managers
- review learner progress
- produce reports for IQAs, supervisors or employers.

ACTIVITY

Whichever of the above roles you carry out, how many of the activities listed above are you responsible for? Who carried out the others in the list?

HOW INTERNAL QUALITY ASSURANCE IS CARRIED OUT [6317 unit 401 AC1.1]

The ways in which internal quality assurance is implemented can differ greatly from one organisation to another.

There may be only one person involved in managing and carrying out the process, or there may be many depending on the size, complexity and maturity of the centre.

However, whichever model is used, it can be separated into four main areas of activity:

- documenting, planning and implementing an internal quality assurance system
- planning, supporting and monitoring learning delivery and assessment
- supporting tutor and/or assessor performance
- recording and information management.

DOCUMENTING, PLANNING AND IMPLEMENTING AN INTERNAL QUALITY ASSURANCE SYSTEM

This is a key part of the process, and yet many IQAs report that in their centres little importance is attached to this part of the role, and they have insufficient time in which to properly fulfil the AO requirements.

This aspect of the role includes ensuring that:

- there are written procedures or a policy or strategy for coherent internal quality assurance in the organisation
- a rationale exists, on which the sample plan is based
- there is an internal quality assurance plan in place
- risk in the training and assessment processes is identified, assessed and managed
- all samples are planned and carried out on the basis of the rationale and the assessed risk
- a range of sampling techniques are employed in the sample
- internal quality assurance activities are reviewed to ensure that they continue to measure effectiveness and efficiency
- all liaison with EQAs is positive and constructive

- externally imposed actions are acted on, such as those arising from an EQA monitoring visit
- appeals and complaints from learners are processed appropriately.

WRITTEN PROCEDURES

One of the basic tenets of quality assurance is that you state what you intend to do – compliance with this can then be monitored. In learning, this usually means that the centre has written procedures (sometimes called a policy or strategy) that describe what its internal quality assurance system consists of, who does what and how it is managed.

These procedures may be in one or a series of documents but they will cover the aims for the system and how they will be implemented and reviewed. They have a variety of other uses, too – for example, they are very useful in outlining for visitors or new members of staff exactly how the centre runs. EQAs find them very helpful. They can also form the basis of induction for new staff and provide a way of ensuring that all team members have the correct documentation.

The basic principles of quality assurance are:

- *State what you are going to do*
- *Do it*
- *Monitor that it's being done*
- *Prove it*

The written procedures should include:
- A description of how the centre is managed – for example, they may include an organisation chart with reporting lines and teams identified. They often include a description of how team members are trained, monitored and communicate.
- Rationales for sampling and an outline of how sampling strategies are decided. They may describe how the centre assesses risk and then what actions are taken to manage it (see page 41 for further details).
- How the sample planning process is organised and carried out. This may include details of the format that the plan(s) will take, who completes the documents, when this is done, where the documents are stored, how they will be used and maintained and how access is restricted. They often include an example of the planning document(s) that will be used.
- A description of which sampling methods will be used, eg observations of practice, discussions with witnesses, examination of records (see page 43 for further details).
- An explanation of how basic administration systems will be organised and maintained – including details of how databases are kept up to date and how learners' work will be held in secure storage.
- A description of assessment and quality assurance systems/documentation and how it will be organised and maintained. Some procedures append examples of assessment and documentation with guidance notes as to how they are typically used.
- Descriptions of the roles of tutors, assessors and IQAs and an outline of the recruitment process.

- The assessment strategy (if appropriate) that team members need to comply with, and an outline of the minimum skills, knowledge and competence required of team members – tutors, assessors and IQA staff – to meet the assessment strategy.
- An overall explanation of how team members' practice will be monitored, supported and developed. Again the documents to be used would often be appended.
- A description of how assessor consistency will be maintained. This may include a description of scheduled team meetings, IQA observation of team members working with learners, types of standardisation activities undertaken, etc.
- A description of the CPD planning and recording process. In some centres an annual Training Needs Analysis (TNA) process is used to ensure that team members continue to meet the requirements of the qualifications that they are delivering. This would be described in the procedures.
- How the performance outcomes for assessment and internal quality assurance (such as figures and statistics) will be recorded and monitored.
- A process for ensuring regular (usually annual) review and a measure of version control to ensure that documents can be controlled and easily identified as the current version.

They might also include an annual plan with dates of team meetings, observations, support sessions, programme reviews, etc.

An extract from an organisation's internal quality assurance procedures can be found in Appendix 4.

For further information on records and systems, see page 74: Recording and information management.

For further information on supporting assessors, see page 60.

ACTIVITY

Get a copy of the internal quality assurance procedure (it may be called a policy or strategy) for your centre. Does the document provide a description of all the areas listed above? Is the entire role of the IQA outlined?

What is missing?

If you do find that not all the documents are in one place, you could then (diplomatically) ask the QAC or IQAC in your centre where the other documents or details are located.

PLANNING, SUPPORTING AND EVALUATING LEARNING DELIVERY AND ASSESSMENT

DETERMINING THE COMPETENCE OF THE TEAM

When an IQA has been charged with the role of planning the delivery of a programme or qualification, having written the procedures, the next major activity they might need to undertake is to recruit staff or, more often, to determine if existing team members can work on the new programme. There is a wealth of information and material on recruitment in other books and sources, so this book does not cover the detail of a general process, but will explain some of the ways that the IQA might determine the suitability of people to join the team.

The IQA may have to produce role descriptors for the various roles required, eg tutor and assessor roles. These role descriptors would closely follow the set requirements of the programme, or they could be outlined in the assessment strategy for the programme or qualification.

The IQA might then advertise these roles internally and hope for interest to be shown. Alternatively – and again, more often – the IQA will already have people on the team who can meet the requirements for working on the new programmes.

The IQA might request CVs or statements from team members to check how their qualifications, knowledge, skills and abilities meet the specifications in the programme or qualification provided by the AO or other external agency.

The specifications can take many forms and vary greatly in nature. Some requirements are very specific and give time limits; others are more subjective in style and are open to interpretation. For example, a requirement in the guidance material from the AO could be that anyone working on that programme or qualification must:

- already hold the qualification at a higher level than that at which they will be tutoring or assessing
- have prior experience in working on that programme or qualification in a previous role
- have been active in a similar role for one year in the last two
- be qualified as teachers or assessors prior to starting to deliver on the programme
- have 'credible experience' in the vocational field of the programme or qualification.

Check the guidance from the AO about the qualifications and experience that staff need to deliver the programme/qualifications.

So the first action of the IQA would be to ascertain which people meet the specifications. They may examine the CVs and other details provided to them and be able quickly to decide who could legitimately carry out the role. Alternatively, they might need to interview/discuss this further with others involved.

In addition, there may be regulatory requirements (often related to funding) which mean that to join the team people will need to hold certain qualifications and be members of a professional body, such as the Institute for Learning (IfL) in England (see www.ifl.ac.uk). Again, it would be the IQA who determines whether this is necessary and can be met by those interested in the roles.

Sometimes IQAs will use a 'skillscan' to determine if team members can meet the requirements, and these are occasionally provided by the AO. For an example of a skillscan see: http://cdn.cityandguilds.com/ProductDocuments/Learning/Training_and_Development/6317/Additional_documents/6317_TAQA_Generic_Skillscan_v1.pdf

Once this process is complete and the team is in place, the IQA will need to monitor that team members' activities and learning continue to meet the requirements year on year. This is where the planning and recording of CPD is very important. External monitors such as EQAs will often request sight of CPD plans and records, because the programme or qualification may include specific CPD requirements that are detailed and exact, and which must be met in order for the team member to remain appropriate. However, other programmes or qualifications have requirements that are far less prescriptive and more open to interpretation. See page 90 for more about CPD for IQAs.

These CPD requirements can be expressed differently in various sectors, but they will usually be something like one or more of the points below – '….on this programme/qualification anyone involved in teaching or assessing must…':
- attend at least two CPD events each year
- show current evidence of CPD
- carry out 30 hours of hands-on practice in a real workplace every year
- have up-to-date knowledge of best practice
- read relevant journals
- undertake placements in practice situations
- attend relevant conferences.

So the IQA will need to monitor on an annual basis whether team members continue to meet the requirements specified in the guidance – and so can remain on the delivery team. They will also need to keep records demonstrating that the requirements are being met, as these are likely to be requested by the EQA and could possibly be scrutinised by other agencies or inspectors.

SAMPLING [6317 unit 401 AC3.1]

What is an internal quality assurance 'sample'?

You will see that the word 'sampling' occurs throughout the information already provided. Fundamental to the internal quality assurance procedures will be the rationale for sampling and the sampling strategies that are selected and used as a result.

However, before looking at rationales and strategies in detail, it is useful to establish what in this book we mean when we use the term 'sample'.

ACTIVITY – NO CHEATING!

What is a 'sample'?

You have been asked to check that the quality is consistent in 500 chocolate biscuits. They have been produced by five bakers who baked two batches of 50 each.

- Would you bite each biscuit?
- If not, how many would you bite? What do you think would be the minimum number to ensure a 'safe' sample?

See page 218 for answer.

Sampling is not biting every biscuit – nor indeed looking at every training session or assessment document. Attending every session would be intrusive and expensive, and an IQA looking at every document would probably be better termed 'second assessment'.

The term 'sampling' in internal quality assurance means the IQA selects a small number of representative examples of something to scrutinise – rather than looking at everything. However, this smaller number of examples must be carefully selected on a planned and rational basis to ensure that over time they cover everything that must be monitored. This reduced number of examples must also give the IQA confidence that what they are seeing is typical (representative) of what has happened in the entire programme, set, batch or cohort. So it is extremely important that the examples selected are based on a sound rationale – and are therefore representative of that tutor or assessor's work.

In evaluating a tutor's work, the IQA may be the person who plans the sessions, agrees the content of the programme, oversees the materials developed and agrees the assignments set. The IQA takes responsibility for how the programme is both delivered and assessed. Having agreed the outline programme and content, the IQA may then sit in on a number of the planned sessions to monitor the quality of the training delivery. The amount of monitoring carried out will depend upon the assessment of risk that the IQA makes in relation to the programme. Factors that are considered when assessing risk are discussed on page 42 below.

The IQA may also use other methods of monitoring of the tutor's work, such as sampling learners' work, having discussions with the tutor and the learners, or reviewing learner progress overall. All of these techniques are discussed further on page 53.

It is generally agreed that numerical formulae or rationales for sampling assessment decisions do not guarantee a representative sample. Some that were used in the past included:

- percentage sampling, eg selecting 20% of an assessor's work; this rationale may lead to an unrepresentative sample because it might not take into account learners from a range of backgrounds, sites, genders, cohorts, etc, or assessors who may be inexperienced in assessment, lacking in confidence or new to the team, etc
- selecting the sample based on the square root of the number of an assessor's work is unrepresentative for the same reasons.

Sampling depends on having a reasonable rationale on which to decide what to sample, and then selecting from the entire body of work a representation of the assessor's judgements. From this representative sample it is reasonable then to infer that all the assessor's work and judgements are similar, have been made on the basis of evidence that meets the assessment criteria, and are valid, authentic, reliable, current and sufficient.

The basis on which the sample is selected is commonly called the rationale for the sample – this is explored more in the section below.

ACTIVITY – NO PEEKING! [6317 unit 401 AC3.1]

There are a few main types of sampling. What do you think the following terms mean? Try to complete the definitions:

Interim sampling takes place
....

Vertical sampling is where the IQA samples

....

Horizontal sampling is where the IQA samples

....

Theme-based sampling is where the IQA samples

....

Summative sampling takes place

....

Now look at the following definitions.......

See page 218 for answers.

Most people only refer to interim (aka formative) sampling or final (aka summative) sampling when they talk about the different types of sampling. However, as you can see below, these two types of sampling can take a number of different formats.

Interim or formative sampling
This takes place while the learner is still on the programme and the programme has not yet been completed by the group or cohort. On new programmes, or with inexperienced assessors, it is often carried out after a short period of time. On a one-year programme, for example, it might take place two months into the programme or when the learners have completed two units of the qualification. If a qualification, tutor or assessor is giving cause for concern, there may be further interim samples – perhaps as many as one every two months. Then there may be a review of the experience and findings at the end of the programme.

This sampling method is designed to ensure that everything is progressing as planned. The outcome from interim/formative sampling may then be used to 'form', develop or change the programme – hence the name.

This is one of the main benefits of interim sampling, and why it is so dear to AOs – it can identify problems early enough in the programme for them to be rectified and not replicated before the programme has progressed too far. So in many ways it is a safety valve in the process. Monitoring activity early and making adjustments is a very powerful tool for improving practice and for ensuring quality.

Final or summative sampling

As the name suggests, this takes place towards or at the end of a programme or qualification. It tends to be where the IQA checks that actions identified in previous samples have been carried out, that everything is in place and the learner has done everything necessary to complete. It must always take place before a certificate is claimed, as this sample 'authenticates' the claim (see City & Guilds, 'Our Quality Assurance Requirements', March 2011 Version 1.0, page 15).

It is 'summative' as it is a 'summing up' of the quality checks that have taken place. Hopefully – if a suitable amount of interim sampling has been completed and appropriate actions taken – there will be no surprises for anyone as a result of the final sampling process.

Vertical sampling

This is most often planned for and carried out during interim sampling. The IQA will sample one unit or learning outcome across all the learners and all the assessors. This enables a comparison to be made between how different tutors and/or assessors are delivering the same unit to different learners in different locations. It is a good way of identifying consistencies – or inconsistencies – in approach, working methods, decision making and feedback.

Horizontal sampling

This is the most commonly used type of internal quality assurance sampling. Over a period of time the IQA plans and samples something from every unit or learning outcome across a qualification or programme. It results in an overall picture of how things are progressing, and can then be supplemented by additional samples if issues are identified. On large qualifications with many units or modules, it may take more than one plan to cover all the units. So an IQA may plan to sample all the mandatory units in one period, then move to sampling the optional units later.

Theme-based sampling

This is only used infrequently by IQAs, as it is a less extensive type of sampling. It tends to be used on stable programmes that have already been subject to a lot of scrutiny and where few issues have been found. Following a series of other forms of sampling, it can be a way of focusing on a particular area of work. With this method, one activity or type of evidence is sampled across tutors, assessors, learners, sites etc – for example, the IQA (having already carried out horizontal sampling) might decide to sample something from the records of observations carried out on a programme. They may select one from each unit of the qualification, across assessors, learners, sites, etc, and look at them as an entity in themselves. This sampling often results in specifically focused development activities for tutors and assessors.

Rationales for selecting a sample [6317 unit 401 AC2.2]

The written internal quality assurance procedures (see page 33) in an organisation will identify the rationale for the sample – this is the basis on which it will be selected. Because of different levels of risk or particular requirements, the sampling strategies planned may differ from programme to programme or from site to site.

City and Guilds uses a tried and tested rationale for selecting the sample of an assessor's work. Its acronym is CAMERA and it states that in order to be fully representative, IQA sampling should include something from all different types of:

- **C**andidates/learners
- **A**ssessors
- **M**ethods of assessment
- **E**vidence
- **R**ecords
- **A**ssessment sites.

Check out the rationale your centre uses with colleagues in addition to examining policy documents.

So when an IQA is starting to consider the size and content of a sample, they would need to take into account these requirements. They would then include each of the following in the plan to ensure a representative sample is selected:

Factor	Need to be sure that the sample covers all types of:
Candidates/learners	Ethnic origin, age, gender, language, any other relevant feature of the candidate/learner population.
Assessors	Experience and qualifications, peripatetic, workload, occupational experience, unqualified/newly qualified/new to centre or team.
Methods of assessment	Questioning, observation, testimony, planned discussion, recognised prior learning (RPL), simulations, examining work products, reflective accounts, marking of projects, assignments, case studies, test, skills tests.
Evidence	All types of evidence – questions, observations, testimonies, written statements, discussions, assignments, projects, work products.
Records	Assessment plans, reports from assessors, documentation recording feedback, reviews of progress, candidate records, certification documents.
Assessment sites	Work environment, training environments, access to support, other assessment locations.

A sample based on this rationale – and covering all the different possibilities in each of the factors – would be fully representative and should cover all quality requirements.

Assessing risk

'Risk' in internal quality assurance is caused by factors or activities that increase the likelihood of something going wrong in the delivery of the programme or qualification.

Even when a system is based on a sound rationale, such as that described above, it is not just a simple process of planning and carrying out the same type or volume of sampling with each programme, cohort of learners or qualification.

When planning the sample – based on the rationale – a range of risk factors need to be considered, as these will determine what type and quantity of sampling should be carried out. The assessment of risk needs to include consideration of factors such as those listed in the table below.

The age, experience, maturity and stability of the organisation

If a centre has been successfully operating the same qualifications with the same staff and has had consistently good feedback from the EQA and others, then the approach to the sample might be a 'light touch'.
However, if it is a relatively new centre with staff who have not delivered qualifications before and there has already been a change of assessor, then the sample may need to be considerably increased – and take place earlier in the process of the qualification.

The size of organisation – how many learners on each programme or qualification?

If a centre delivers only one or two qualifications from the same occupational area, and has only 20 learners in total, then the risk is limited – so the internal quality assurance might be less extensive.
However, if a centre has a total of 17,500 learners on 30 different qualifications from 8 different occupational sectors, then the risk is somewhat increased. The nature and amount of the quality assurance at this centre would be different and much greater than at the smaller centre.

The complexity or sophistication of the organisation

The way the organisation is structured can increase or reduce risk. Larger organisations with multi-layer management structures are obviously more at risk than smaller, flatter, more transparent ones. So the internal quality assurance plan would reflect the complexity of the centre.
However, if the complex organisation is broken down into well-defined departments with clear and accountable reporting channels and has tutor, assessor and IQA roles that are detailed, carried out on a routine basis and understood by all, then the risk is reduced. In this situation individual departments would be likely to manage their own quality assurance.

The number of qualifications, levels and locations

Centres that deliver a large range of qualifications at a variety of levels are obviously more of a risk, as outlined above. This risk can be increased considerably if the organisation is split over a number of sites. This often happens when two or more centres merge or go into partnership. The planning must then cover all sites, and may identify trends in some locations that do not exist in others – therefore as the risk increases, the planned internal quality assurance would need to reflect this.

Obviously, a greater number of tutors and assessors results in a proportionate increase in risk. In addition, the more tutors and assessors who work on the programme or qualification, the more observations are required – possibly resulting in more meetings being held, more annual staff TNAs to be processed, etc. So the amount of work carried out by the IQA will increase proportionately.

The experience and confidence of the tutors and assessors

In many situations people gain experience at the same rate but increase in confidence at a very different rate. Some tutors are completely at ease having delivered a programme once, while others may have delivered the same programme three or more times before they feel confident. There is an increased risk of problems arising where tutors lack confidence – if nothing else, they are likely to need additional support from the IQA. So once again the level and type of internal quality assurance planned and carried out would need to be responsive to these needs and suited to the individual.

Exactly the same situation can arise with assessors – some feel confident as soon as they are familiar with the qualification they are assessing. Others are apprehensive about taking assessment decisions and so may over-assess for a period. This could be unfair to their learners and can be costly and time-consuming. It is essential that the IQA identifies what is happening and then plans additional IQA sampling. The assessor may also need additional support, such as having one-to-one sessions with the IQA or shadowing another assessor.

The numbers and experience of IQAs

There is an increased risk of problems where a number of IQAs work on the same qualification, or even in the same centre on different qualifications. One of the purposes of internal quality assurance is to ensure consistency. Therefore where there is a team of IQAs, the QAC will need to plan to sample their work to ensure that they are using the same systems and making quality assurance decisions on a coherent basis. Also, this enables the QAC to ensure that the feedback being given to the tutors and assessors by the IQAs is similar in type, nature and amount. The same factors we saw in the sampling of assessors apply here – the numbers of IQAs, their skills, abilities, levels of experience and confidence would impact on the amount of sampling that the QAC carries out.

In addition, a team of IQAs may share out the sampling that the centre does, and the risk assessments that they undertake will depend upon factors related specifically to their sample.

New, inexperienced IQAs who lack confidence will often over-sample (some look at every page of every piece of a learner's work!) and may even begin to re-assess. This is not practical, efficient or effective – in fact, it ceases to be a sample and becomes just a second assessor signature. Once again, the QAC needs to identify that this is happening and intervene to support and guide the inexperienced IQAs to plan and sample appropriately.

Independent assessment (required in some qualifications only)

There are requirements in some qualifications for a proportion of the learner's work to be assessed by someone other than the primary or main assessor. In this situation the work that has been independently assessed must be included on the plan and sampled by the IQA. Independent assessment may pose an increased risk to the qualification, because very often the assessor is not as immersed in the qualification as the primary assessor would be, and there is a risk of inconsistency in judgements and feedback.

Any dispersed assessment locations, satellites, partnerships or consortia arrangements

Any centre that has more than one site poses an increased risk of differences in training and assessment practice taking place, inconsistent assessment decisions being made and, in general, of maverick tutor and/or assessor behaviour. In addition to these risks, partnership and consortia arrangements mean that all partners may already have assessment and internal quality assurance systems and practice in place which they consider to be effective. These systems can conflict and may actually promote inconsistent practice – this can be a very uncomfortable situation for an IQA.

The most positive way forward is for the centre to plan for increased activity by the QAC or Quality Manager. To work towards controlling the risk, they need to take responsibility for harmonising the systems and practices and producing one set of procedures for the entire (new) organisation. This can have the effect of cementing relationships and working practices rather than causing rifts. In addition, during this harmonisation process it is important that risk is minimised by increased sampling by the individual IQAs assigned to the programmes or qualifications. A further concern or risk in this process lies in who is ultimately responsible for the systems and activities that take place, and who is accountable when the system fails to fulfil its functions.

Changes in the qualifications that are imminent or have already taken place

A proactive IQA will keep abreast of developments in their occupational areas, programmes and qualifications and ensure that preparation work is done with and by the team of tutors and assessors prior to the changes being introduced.

Therefore, to reduce risk, increased IQA activity would be planned even before the changes take place. Then when the new arrangements have been implemented there will be a need for early and increased IQA sampling of the training delivery, support given to learners and assessment decisions taken. This will help to ensure that practices are accurate and in line with requirements before the programme has progressed to a point where it is difficult – if not impossible – to put them right.

Known problem areas in qualifications – such as particular issues with a unit

Many qualifications have units, assignments or individual criteria that perennially cause problems for assessors. This poses an additional risk. The problems can exist for a wide range of reasons – some of which may be individual and unique to the centre. It is very useful for the IQA to increase the amount of sampling of these areas and make them the subject of standardisation activities and team meetings.

Use of new technology

Technology is having an increasing impact on learning. If tutors and assessors are using a particular piece of technology with which they are unfamiliar, such as an e-portfolio or delivering support sessions by webinar for the first time, then just due to a lack of experience the risk level is raised. This situation may result in the IQA arranging training sessions with team members, 'attending' webinars to monitor activity and undertaking additional sampling in the case of e-portfolios.

This is not a finite list of risks that an IQA might have to assess before planning their sample. What additional risks might you need to take into consideration?

It is very important that when the IQA has completed the risk assessment, they then plan their sample and use the most effective techniques for whatever they are going to monitor.

INTERNAL QUALITY ASSURANCE PLANNING

[6317 unit 401 AC2.1 & 2.2]

The sample plan

So having considered the rationale, carried out the risk assessment and selected which techniques they will use to sample, the IQA then writes up what they are going to do in an internal quality assurance sample plan.

The sample plan might be stored electronically or on paper. It could be one overarching document for a centre, or a series of smaller ones (for example, one for each department) stored in a number of places. In many ways the documentation used is irrelevant, as long as it serves the purpose of allowing the IQA to plan their sample (having assessed the risk, based their plan on the rationale and decided on the type of sampling....) and record what they have done. It is useful to remember that in many centres each plan is likely to be individual to the particular group or cohort of learners, team, qualification and indeed IQA.

In many centres the sample plan document will also be used to record the sampling undertaken. So the document may convert from being a plan to being a record as soon as it is used. As long as the people using it understand the difference between what is being planned and the record of the sample having taken place, then there is no problem with this.

The IQA will include most of the following in the plan:

- the assessor names
- learner names
- the units or sections in the programme or qualification
- the units or sections of the programme or qualification that they are going to sample
- rough dates when they plan to carry out the sample.

Below are some examples of planning documents.

'Plans are nothing; planning is everything.' Dwight D. Eisenhower

Ask an experienced colleague to explain how your centre's own plan is used.

Internal Quality Assurance Sampling Plan/Record

Qualification title: WBD Level2 **Qualification number:** 0022 02

Internal Verifier(s): V Sethbury **Assessor(s):** H Choo

Candidate/learner Names:	Unit 1	Unit 2	Unit 3	Unit 4	Unit 5	Unit 6	Unit 7	Unit 8	Unit	Unit	Summative Date
Alison Hong	F 11/11										Nov 2012
Fay Harper				F 01/12							Nov 2012
Vikram Anaahat						F 02/12					Nov 2012
Sind Budhdev		F 11/11									Nov 2012
Annette Denton							F O 02/12				Nov 2012
Josh McCormack			F 12/11								Nov 2012
Rosetta Dawasatti								F 03/12			Nov 2012
Jack Parker					F 01/12						Nov 2012

Please enter dates of actual internal sampling.

KEY F = Formative S = Summative O = Observation

Page 47 shows a simple planning document where the IQA has selected horizontal sampling across the units in the qualification and across learners for one assessor. She has identified the unit that she is going to sample for each learner and the month it will take place. She has also planned when she is going to undertake an observation. She has set a projected date for when she plans to carry out a final check – towards the end of the programme. When she starts the sample, she will then convert this document to an ongoing record of her sampling. On page 48 you will find that the plan has now been implemented – and the document has become a record of the sampling undertaken.

ACTIVITY

If all sample plans should be based on the acronym CAMERA (see page 41) – what factors from CAMERA are missing from this plan?

See page 218 for answer.

Internal Quality Assurance Sampling Plan/Record

Qualification title: WBD Level2

Qualification number: 0022 02

Internal Verifier(s): V Sethbury

Assessor(s): H Choo

Candidate/ Learner Names:	Unit 1	Unit 2	Unit 3	Unit 4	Unit 5	Unit 6	Unit 7	Unit 8	Summative Date
Alison Hong	F 28/11/10								15/06/11
Fay Harper				F 31/11/10					21/06/11
Vikram Anaahat						F 16/12/10			15/06/11
Sind Budhdev		F 12/1/11							15/06/11
Annette Claas							F/O 12/11/10		21/06/11
Josh Mc Cormack			F 15/2/11						15/06/11
Rosetta Dawasatti								F 10/03/11	21/06/11
Jack Parker					F 15/3/07				21/06/11
Jez Canterbury									15/06/11

Please enter dates of actual internal sampling.

KEY   F = Formative   S = Summative   O = Observation

Page 48 shows the same plan which has now become a record as it has been completed with the actual dates when the sampling took place. It also now contains the date of the final or summative 'sign off' of the learner's work. As you can see, the summative dates differ as some learners completed slightly before others, or the IQA checked some on different dates to others.

On page 50 you will find is a more complex plan/record that tries to meet all the requirements of CAMERA. In addition to the previous plan, this one includes:
- a categorisation of the assessors
- a categorisation of the learners
- the units or sections of the programme or qualification that they are going to sample
- the evidence that they plan to sample.

INTERNAL QUALITY ASSURANCE SAMPLING PLAN/RECORD

IQA Name: M Southall

Qualification: Retail L2

Assessor Names	Assessor Category	Candidate Name	Type of Cand	Units to be Sampled (Shade when completed)			IQA Dates (projected month & actual date shaded)	Evidence to be sampled (shade when sampled)	Assessment Site
M McCarthy	E/P/Q	Charlotte Williams	F/E/N	Unit 1	Unit 2	Op	28.03.11 06.06.11 Sept 2011	QU/AR/IA/WT	Kind Care Ltd
M McCarthy	E/P/Q	Mia Bogdanovic	F/E	Unit 1		Op	06.06.11 Sept 2011	OB/PA/CR/DA	Wellbeing[en] Social Serv
Z Smyth	E/P/Q	Jed Khan	M/E	Unit 1		Op	06.06.11 Sept 2011	WT/PR/CR/QU	Wellbeing Social Serv
Z Smyth	E/P/Q	Gaby Ponsetta	F/E	Unit 1		Op	06.06.11 Sept 2011	QU/AR/ IA/WT	Wellbeing Social Serv

Sampling activity key
QU = Questioning
AR = Assessment Records Examined
IA = Independent Assessment

WT = Witness Testimony
OB = Observation of Assessment
PA = Project / Assignment
OP = Optional Unit

CR = Candidate Report
DA = Discussion with Assessor
DW = Discussion with Witness

RPL = Recognised Prior Learning
PR = Product Evidence Sampled
PD = Planned Discussion

Assessor Categories:

Experienced	- E
Probationary	- Prob
Primary	- PR
Independent	- IN
Peripatetic	- P
Work Based	- W
Qualified	- Q

Cand/Learner Categories:

Male	- M
Female	- F
Employed	- E
Unemployed	- U

Candidate/Learner category:

Government Training Scheme	- G
Special Assessment Requirements	- S
Night Shift Worker	- N
Welsh Speaker	- W
Speaker of another language	- O
Voluntary Worker	- V

As you can see, in the plan/record on page 50 the IQA has sampled horizontally across two assessors and vertically by sampling Unit 1 throughout. The IQA will also sample from the optional units in the qualification. The IQA has changed the prospective month of the sample identified on the plan to an actual date and highlighted the date once the sample has been completed.

ACTIVITY

On the last plan, what do you notice about what the IQA has planned to sample and then carried out? Why do you think they did that?

Are there any factors required by CAMERA missing from this plan? How could this plan be improved?

See page 218 for answers.

Qualification: H&SC 0234

Standardisation unit: Unit 1 (Communication) across all learners

Name of IQA: M Sayce

Assessor	Assessor Status	Assessment Site	Candidates/ Learners	Units that have been assessed. Units to be sampled by the IQA according to the sampling plan are shaded. Any variations from the plan are in bold								Part of the assessment process reviewed	Method of assessment checked
A Horsley	Q	Leeds	L2 TS	1	2	3	4	5	6			1. DO/EWT 2. WP	P / R
			L3 AG	1	2	3	4	5	6	7	8	DO/EWT S	P / R
			L4 RA	1	2	3	4	5	6	7	8	DO/EWT RPL	P / R
B Quinton	Q	Bradford	L2 AX	1	2	3	4	5	6			DO/EWT PD	P / R
			L2 BX	1	2	3	4	5	6			DO/EWT	P / R
C Andam	NSQ	Barnsley	L2 QC	1	2	3	4	5	6			DO/EWT	P / R
			L3 JK	1	2	3	4	5	6			DO/EWT	P / RFC
			L3 MS	1	2	3	4	5	6	7	8	DO/EWT	P / F

Key -
planned sampling
additional sampling until assessor confident re: centre practices

Page 52 shows a City & Guilds example of a more complex plan based on the same principle as the previous one. It includes vertical sampling of Unit 1 and then horizontal sampling across units and learners.

In addition to the previous plans, this one also includes:
- the level of qualification that each learner is undertaking
- a mechanism for recording additional sampling undertaken.

Having planned the sample, the IQA then needs to store the information safely and restrict access to it. It is important that tutors and assessors are not aware of what is going to be sampled, though they may know roughly when they can expect it to happen. So, for example, they may know that they need to collect the candidate's work and deliver it to the IQA in a particular week, but they would not know which section/unit/piece of work was going to be sampled.

This is important, as it is only natural that tutors and assessors want to be well respected, and so if they knew what was going to be sampled they may – even unwittingly – skew their work or decisions to ensure that what the candidate did in that unit was of a particularly good standard. In addition, they might double-check their paperwork to make sure that there are no omissions, when this is not something they would normally do. The sample would not be typical of that tutor or assessor's work – and so would not be representative.

Therefore, access to the IQA plan/record, although a working document, must be restricted to authorised people only and the document must not be on general display.

SAMPLING ACTIVITIES [6317 unit 401 AC3.1]

As you can see from the section on planning above, it is really important that when the IQA has completed the risk assessment they then plan well. Part of this planning should include consideration of which activity or technique best 'fits' whatever they are going to sample. So they may select and plan to use different techniques in order to carry out an effective sample of different activities.

The outcomes and feedback from each technique also provide mechanisms for supporting the tutors and assessors. So, for example, reporting back to the tutor or assessor about a discussion held with a learner (who has given permission for the information to be relayed) may provide useful feedback for them. Here are some of the most commonly used IQA sampling techniques.

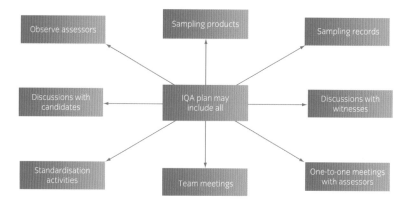

Inevitably, different techniques are better with some types of work than others. For example, observation, consideration of session plans and discussions with learners are probably the most effective techniques for sampling a tutor's work.

However, a standardisation activity might be a better way of sampling a theme in a programme, such as how well assessors are recording observations. So the IQA has to give consideration to what they are aiming to find out and select the IQA technique that is going to give them the greatest insight into the work.

These are the ways in which the various techniques are mainly used:

Observation of assessors
This is used by the IQA to monitor the interaction and rapport between the tutor or assessor and their learners, to ensure that the staff member is carrying out the process in a systematic and clear way, that they are completing the required documentation, to ensure that they give appropriate feedback, respond to questions from the learners and finally that they agree suitable forward action plans with them.

How it's done
The IQA will produce a checklist of what they are expecting to see during the observation – this could be based on content from the Assessment and Quality Assurance units or from the Learning and Development units according to which function they are observing (see Appendices 5, 6, 7 and 8 for examples of checklists). They would talk through what they are looking for with the tutor or assessor beforehand, then carry out the observation. Following the observation, they would start the feedback to the tutor/assessor by asking them how they thought they had performed, and then methodically talk through everything that they had recorded on the checklist. Depending on what was observed, they may agree an action plan with target dates for improvements to be made.

Sampling products

This technique is used for ensuring that learners are making expected progress, that they are producing what is required by the programme or qualification, that their work is valid, that the assessment decisions taken about the work are accurate, that the feedback being given about the work is appropriate and helpful, and that any necessary further development has been planned.

How it's done

Different centre models result in various issues with the practicalities of getting work in from learners, tutors and assessors in order to carry out planned sampling activities. Be assured that everything that can go wrong does!

A planned sample of products means that near the date for the sample the IQA needs to request the learner's work and related records from the tutor or assessor and prepare the paperwork – such as any checklists or feedback forms – access the plan, possibly book a room, etc, in readiness for the sampling activity. Then the learner's work, records and documents all need to be in the same location as the IQA – this is far more difficult to achieve than it sounds on paper! These are some of the typical things that can go wrong:

- the tutor/assessor and learners forget about the planned sample altogether
- learners do not deliver the work to the tutor or assessor as planned
- learners have not completed the work/unit that was expected by that date, so the planned sample cannot take place and an alternative unit/module or type of work has to be selected; alternatively the sample could be postponed
- the tutor/assessor leaves the learner's work at home, where they have been assessing it
- the IQA goes to an agreed location (for example to observe the assessor working) and for legitimate reasons the venue has been changed by the assessor and learner; however, no one has informed the IQA
- witnesses who had agreed to meet the IQA as part of the sample do not turn up or are not available when contacted.

Once the IQA has overcome these issues, the sample begins. Some IQAs sit together in a room and sample learners' work and assessment decisions together. This is particularly helpful when an IQA is inexperienced or lacking in confidence, or when a new programme or qualification is being sampled for the first time. However, it can be expensive if continued over a long period.

In this sampling technique, the IQA looks at what the learner has produced and what decisions and feedback they have been given by their tutor/assessor in relation to that work. They then check that the requirements of the programme or qualification have been met. They prepare written feedback for the tutor/assessor and complete any other centre records.

This is the same process whether sampling takes place on an interim or final basis. The IQA then completes any externally required records and brings the sample plan (which is now serving as a record) up to date.

If the sample is a formative or interim one, the IQA will take this into consideration and recognise that understandably some of what is required may not yet have been completed.

If the sample is a summative or final one, the IQA will also carry out a final check of the work to ensure that all signatures and dates are included and all recording requirements have been met.

If this is a summative sample and all requirements are met, the IQA then finally 'signs off' the work as complete, signing and dating to own the decision that they have taken, and filling in any necessary documentation to request that a certificate be claimed. This process is known by City & Guilds as 'authentication' and it must be carried out 'by an appropriately occupationally qualified IQA' (City & Guilds, 'Our Quality Assurance Requirements', March 2011, Version 1.0).

If this is an interim sample, the learner's work then is returned to them and feedback given to the tutor/assessor. If this is a final sample then the work may need to be returned to be sampled by an EQA or other representative of the AO.

Sampling records
This is a useful way of ensuring that tutors and assessors are maintaining required records showing that learners are attending as planned, making progress and submitting work as expected. It can also highlight whether feedback is being recorded and, when required, further action is being planned and then reviewed with the learner.

How it's done

The IQA will access the records that the tutor and assessor have been completing, and will monitor the quality of the content. This should involve checking that more than one version of the records of assessment decisions are kept. It is a requirement that at least two copies of the records of assessment decisions should be maintained – one with the learner's work and one in the centre. However, assessors sometimes also like to keep a copy – in case they need access to it when they are away from their workplace. For example, if a learner contacts the assessor with a query about an agreed action, the assessor may find it helpful to have the related document to hand. The IQA will check that the required documents are up to date, stored appropriately and that the content and detail of the records is of a good standard and meets the requirements.

Discussion with witnesses

This is a very useful technique for gaining additional information about the learner and, indeed, the assessor's performance. It is also a way of checking the authenticity of a learner's work and gaining reassurance about the integrity of the work. This can sometimes help the IQA to confirm assessment judgements and contextualise the feedback being given to the learner by the tutor/assessor.

How it's done

When sampling work products, the IQA identifies where other people have contributed to the process – for example, where witness or even expert witness statements have been used. Where witness statements are used as a source of evidence, the learner should include contact details for the witnesses in their work.

The IQA makes contact with the witness and asks them about the statements that they have made. The sampling of the work products may have raised specific questions or points for the IQA that need to be explained or clarified by the witness. Alternatively, the IQA may ask the witness probing questions, such as, 'How would you describe the way CG carried out *specific activity* when you were working with him?' The IQA will record what the witness says and keep a copy of the record in the centre.

The IQA will often later discuss what the witness reported with the tutor and/or assessor. In many cases, a discussion with a witness can help to cement an IQA decision. Many witnesses are far more generous in their praise of a learner verbally than they are when expressing comments on paper. In addition, the IQA can ask the witness for comments on their impression of the assessor or tutor.

One-to-one meetings with team members

This method allows an IQA to look in detail at the work completed by the tutor or assessor or to discuss and confirm decisions taken. It is also a great form of support for team members. Some centres schedule in such meetings on a bi-monthly or quarterly basis to give both parties a formal mechanism and 'time out' to consider topics such as workload, problem areas (or learners), to look at learner work together, discuss CPD requirements, areas where they are experiencing difficulty, etc.

How it's done

The IQA produces a plan for the support that they will make available to the tutors or assessors. This plan is often produced on an annual basis (see page 68 for an example of what such a plan might look like and contain). On the plan they will schedule one-to-one meetings with the tutors/assessors. These can take a range of formats but should always have an agenda and a record kept of what was discussed and what actions are to be taken by whom and by when.

Team meetings

These provide an opportunity for team members to get together, receive updates, reflect on progress, consider issues, discuss feedback from the EQA, plan for the future as a team, etc. This is separate from and different to a standardisation activity, though standardisation activities often take place after a team meeting is concluded.

How it's done

If the IQA produces an annual support plan, then it is easy to include team meetings (see page 68 for an example plan). As with most meetings, if they are planned well in advance then team members are more likely to be able to attend. Also, a formal process should be followed that includes the circulation of an agenda prior to the meeting and minutes being kept. It is always a good idea when meetings are planned in advance for the chairperson to send a reminder out to participants a few days or even a week ahead of the date. Some IQAs have a set agenda for their meetings, then they add topical points to it just prior to circulating the meeting reminder (see Appendix 10 for a typical team meeting agenda).

Standardisation activities

If the IQA plans well, this can be a very useful method of sampling that allows team members to focus on specific areas of work. It can make use of peer review and feedback and result in team members voluntarily changing their practice. Additionally, it can provide the IQA with reasons why the tutor and assessor practice should change (see page 69 for more detail and an outline of possible standardisation activities).

When centres carry out all their assessment internally (as opposed to work being assessed by the AO), there is often a requirement that the assessment decisions taken by assessors in the centre must be standardised. Therefore standardisation activities are a useful method of sampling, and holding them meets one of the requirements set by the AO.

How it's done

If the IQA or IQAC produces an annual support plan, then once again it is also relatively easy to include standardisation activities (see page 68 for an IQAC support plan). The activity may be part of a team meeting, carried out immediately after a team meeting or indeed be held on a separate date. There are a range of possible standardisation activities already in existence (see page 69). It is true to say that most IQAs are interested in innovative ways of developing consistency among their team members, and are open to new ideas for activities that will result in standardised approaches and practice.

Discussions with learners

'The proof of the pudding is in the eating' is a very true saying – sometimes to really find out about the quality of the work being delivered by team members it is most effective to talk directly to the consumers of that work. Learners will often tell the IQA (as an objective third party) things that they would not divulge to their tutor or assessor. They should be able to provide information on why issues have arisen, why target dates have been missed and give detailed feedback about the support they are receiving – or not, as the case may be. Obviously, the IQA will need to use their judgement about the information they are provided with and be sensitive to any underlying motives or issues that may exist.

How it's done

In a similar way to the 'discussions with others', this needs to be planned and recorded by the IQA. Though it may need to be managed in a sensitive and informal manner, this is another legitimate, formal IQA sampling process. It needs to be treated as such, because in addition to its quality assurance function it may form part of other formal processes in the future. It requires that the IQA arranges to meet the learners with a series of prepared questions to prompt the discussion. Where learners lack confidence, it can be better to carry out the discussions in a group – especially if they have been attending sessions together. However, sometimes – and on some qualifications – it works best when carried out one-to-one with the learner. A summary of what the learner says should be recorded, even if only in skeleton notes. Then, with the learner's permission, these can be discussed with others – including their tutor or assessor.

All of these techniques can be planned into the annual quality assurance cycle by the IQA. In some centres they may be recorded on one sample plan – though the information may prove difficult to fit onto one document – and so many IQAs produce a separate quality plan outlining the techniques that do not form part of their routine sampling regime. See page 68 for an example of this additional plan.

SUPPORTING TUTOR AND ASSESSOR PERFORMANCE

MAKING DECISIONS – JUDGING QUALITY

[6317 unit 401 AC3.2]

Find out what your learners have experienced and include this in your thinking about quality.

This is perhaps the most difficult part of the internal quality assurance process to describe. It brings together all the experience and knowledge of the IQA and focuses it on what the tutor or assessor has done and whether it meets requirements and maintains the quality and integrity of what is being delivered.

The decision-making process mainly occurs during or following sampling, and obviously before feedback is given.

When sampling, the IQA will often use a series of documents – such as the observation checklists or an IQA report form – to give feedback to their tutors and/or assessors (see Appendix 11). They will decide – based on what they find in the sample – whether the overall programme delivered:

- has been properly planned
- follows the syllabus/course outline
- is in line with requirements
- utilises a range of training methods
- meets the learners' needs
- encourages learner participation
- has been evaluated.

And monitor that the learning delivery:

- conforms to internal requirements
- meets the AO requirements
- demonstrates good practice
- includes suitable records being kept
- contains areas where the tutor requires further development.

In relation to assessment, in the same way the IQA will decide – based on what they find in the sample – whether assessment decisions are:

- properly planned
- based on judgements against criteria
- safe

- accurate
- based on VARCS (Valid, Authentic, Reliable, Current, Sufficient)
- fully recorded and include agreed further action if necessary.

And the IQA will monitor that the assessment decisions:
- conform to internal requirements
- meet the AO requirements
- demonstrate good practice
- contain areas where the assessor needs to develop.

At some point during the sampling processes the IQA will decide whether they feel that the tutor has met the requirements, and whether they agree with the assessment decision. They will then plan their feedback to the tutor or assessor based on this.

Although the process aims to be as objective as possible – using criteria and specifications to judge against – the IQA decision is inevitably a subjective one that depends a great deal on the previous experience and knowledge of the IQA. It also depends on the culture of the team and the standards of performance that they or their organisation have developed and expect of others.

ACTIVITY

If a centre has high expectations in certain areas – for example, that team members always maintain detailed records – then when a member of that team keeps less detailed records this will be deemed unacceptable by the IQA. In another centre where less detailed records may be the norm this would not be picked up by the IQA as 'not meeting the requirements'.

What words would you use to describe the culture in the first centre as opposed to that in the second?

See page 219 for answers.

Whatever judgements or decisions the IQA takes, it is extremely important that they can justify what they say – whether about learning delivery or assessment judgements. To prepare for this, the IQA can rehearse in their mind how they would explain their decision to someone other than the relevant tutor or assessor, such as the QAC, or an outside person, such as the EQA.

It is only by being able to justify what they have said and done that the IQA will be able to defend the decision if challenged. It is also useful to remember at this point that the challenge may not arise immediately, and so once again it is vital that sufficiently detailed records are kept in order that decisions can be explained if a query should arise in the future.

In a summative (final) sample, the IQA decision may be that the tutor or assessor has made an error or omission and as a result the learner has not fully completed the programme or met all the requirements. In this situation the IQA decision may result in the tutor or assessor having to return to the learner and request further work from them. Learners do not always immediately accept this feedback. Therefore, sometimes the challenge to the IQA decision comes from the learner and not the team member. Once again, as long as the IQA is clear about why they have made the decision and can explain the rationale, then this generally satisfies the person raising the issue. Though they may not be happy with the additional work they need to complete, nor agree with the decision, they will understand why it was taken.

Although this is unusual, the learner could appeal against the IQA's decision and invoke the organisation's appeal procedure (see page 77 for more on appeals).

Also at some point in the process the IQA will make a judgement about the 'quality' of what the tutor or assessor has done. In previous sections we looked briefly at quality – it is difficult to pin down exactly what it is in relation to learning. Is it when learners achieve quickly, or is it when they learn a great deal? Is quality the reason why attendance levels are excellent for some learning delivery sessions – or is it because the learners need the qualification? Quality is quite difficult to quantify for individual programmes, cohorts or qualifications.

For many people the definition 'Getting it right – first time and every time' comes close to the idea of quality, or we might say that something is 'fit for purpose'. However, in 'learning' quality is often much less tangible than these phrases imply.

Most IQAs – like most consumers – know when they have seen quality and clearly know when it is missing. It might be visible where a tutor has engaged the learners to a point at which they are initiating their own work, or where guidance to a learner has resulted in work of a much higher standard than expected, or it could be detailed and specific record keeping that has resulted in an issue being resolved. If something meets or exceeds expectations and has additional beneficial features, then surely it is an example of quality.

ACTIVITY

What does quality practice look like in your role? If you are already involved in IQA sampling, think about a time when you saw good quality in learning delivery or assessment. What was it about the activity that made it stand out as an example of quality?

Where an IQA identifies 'quality', they would complete the required paperwork and give feedback to the tutor or assessor acknowledging their work. If appropriate, they might share the practice that has been identified as being an example of 'quality' with others in the team. It is important that if this is to be done then it is handled sensitively and is a positive experience for everyone, and does not result in some team members feeling that they are not valued.

The example of good practice may also raise the possibility of amending systems or working practices to encourage or support others to improve the quality of their work. It would be the IQA's responsibility to take these opportunities forward to others in the organisation, such as the QAC or Quality Manager, in order to gain agreement for the changes to be made.

Similarly, where they have identified that requirements have not been met, the IQA would fill in the necessary documents and give feedback to the tutor or assessor. Once again, the area for change or development can be shared with others in the team if done sensitively.

Managing this process sensitively may involve the IQA in:
- getting the agreement of the tutor/assessor for the information to be shared
- agreeing with the person concerned that the IQA will raise the issue without exposing which member of the team it relates to
- anonymising the issue and using the principles contained in it as part of a standardisation activity
- using it as an opportunity to consider how everyone's practice can be improved.

'To improve is to change; to be perfect is to change often.'
Winston Churchill

IQA FEEDBACK TO THE TUTOR/ASSESSOR

[6317 unit 401 AC4.1]

Having carried out the sample and identified the good practice (or otherwise) being carried out by team members, the next action that the IQA will take is to provide feedback to the tutor or assessor on the outcome of the sample. This process is sufficiently important – and is often not carried out successfully – that it warrants a closer look.

ACTIVITY

Think of feedback on your performance that you have had in the past. If possible, think of feedback you have had that was given in a negative way and then an instance when you had similar feedback but it was presented in a positive way.

There is a great deal of information already available about giving general feedback in a positive way and about how not to give feedback that is negative in nature. See Appendices 1 and 2 for suggested book and website lists. Many will include information about feedback.

As a 'rule of thumb', the feedback from IQAs to tutors and assessors should follow the same rules of good practice as all other feedback.

Feedback from the IQA to the tutor/assessor should be:	Because...
Honest, clear and detailed	The IQA has to raise all issues they identify with tutors or assessors and give them clear guidance about what to do. IQAs need to have the integrity and confidence to be truthful and to be able to justify and stand by their decisions – even when giving feedback to colleagues or more senior members of staff. Unless the IQA tells the person what has to be changed in a clear and specific way, they will not be able to change and make the necessary improvements.
A dialogue	The tutor/assessor should have an opportunity to reflect on their work before getting the outcome of the sample from the IQA. They should also feel sufficiently 'safe' to put forward their own opinions – even if this may differ from the IQA feedback.
Both written and verbal	Both parties need a record of the outcome of the internal quality assurance. The written record then provides the structure for the feedback as the IQA talks through the record and explains their feedback. Also again this encourages the tutor/assessor to reflect and put forward their opinions.
Constructive and positive	This applies even where there are areas or behaviours that need to change or where inaccuracies or omissions have occurred.
Factual and designed to improve future assessment practice	The tutor/assessor needs to be given specific facts about what they need to do differently or areas where they have omitted data or been inaccurate. In addition, the aim of the feedback is to ensure that the issue or inaccuracy does not get repeated in the person's work.

Feedback from the IQA to the tutor/assessor should be:	Because...
Specific about what has to be done and how it should be done	Most people who get something 'wrong' want to know exactly how to put it 'right'. This may require direct and directive guidance from the IQA and a high level of detail.
Be given in a suitable environment	The feedback is formal, needs to be taken seriously and seen as important by both parties. An indicator of this is the fact that the IQA sets aside sufficient time in an area where the discussion will not be interrupted or overheard – particularly if it is sensitive in nature – and conducts the feedback in a professional manner.
Given in relation to good or excellent practice as well as identifying areas that have not met requirements.	Everyone responds to praise – it is important that IQAs give positive feedback wherever it is deserved. Not giving positive feedback on good performance can result in team members feeling, 'What's the point in trying hard to get it right when it's not recognised anyway?'
Agreed with the tutor/assessor	Any practice or resources that need to be changed should be agreed between the IQA and the tutor/asssessor. Depending on the nature of what has been raised by the IQA, there may be a need to agree action points with timescales.

SUPPORTING TUTOR AND ASSESSOR PERFORMANCE [6317 unit 401 AC4.1]

One of the main ways in which IQAs can improve practice in their centre is by supporting and developing tutor and assessor practice.

Record in detail everything that you agree and undertake with team members.

As mentioned previously, IQAs can use a range of techniques in their sampling, and this also applies to the ways in which they support and develop tutors and assessors. They may undertake a variety of activities including meetings, one-to-one support, annual TNAs, ongoing feedback, standardisation, advice about the content of qualifications, guidance about ways of working, and methods for overcoming issues with learners and the qualifications. In larger centres individual IQAs might carry out only some of these activities, as the QAC, Quality Manager or IQAC would be responsible for others. In smaller centres the IQA would organise and be responsible for all the support provided to the tutors and assessors.

There are many reasons why an IQA needs to carry out these activities. The most effective way that an IQA can effect change and make improvements in practice is by supporting and developing their team. As you have seen on page 53, each of the support mechanisms has benefits, but it is worth pointing out the particular merit of one-to-one meetings.

Though one-to-one meetings are not routinely used by IQAs, dedicated individual time spent with a tutor or assessor is particularly useful as it means that:

- issues can be aired in a 'safe' environment and resolved before they become problems
- areas where the tutor/assessor lacks knowledge, experience or skills can be identified and development needs planned for
- the IQA can give advice, guidance and support to help the tutor/assessor develop
- everyone in the process is kept up to date
- when the IQA identifies actions that an individual tutor or assessor needs to make, these can be discussed confidentially and a way forward agreed
- everyone understands what CPD they need to complete each year.

In any given year the support activities carried out by an IQA may vary and change in type and amount. But once again, risk assessment has a role to play in determining what support is provided to tutors and assessors. If a tutor or assessor is new or lacking in confidence, the IQA will plan in additional sessions with them and might arrange for them to carry out further development activities, such as shadowing more experienced team members.

In reality, in many organisations this support is ad hoc and happens when the IQA realises that a problem has arisen. However, it is far more likely to actually take place, provide an opportunity to pre-empt problems and so have a successful outcome if it is planned in advance, targeted and focused on areas of need, and is part of a larger coherent process of support for team members.

It is useful for IQAs to plan out the formal support that will be taking place on an annual basis. This plan can then be circulated to all team members and anyone else interested in what support is available – such as the Quality Manager or the EQA. It needs to be a dynamic working document that is regularly updated and even supplemented as situations arise. For example, if the IQA had agreed the plan with everyone but then a new tutor joins the team, the activities planned might change or increase in number. Also, if one team member is not able to be observed one month as planned, then the arrangements can be altered to postpone – but not cancel – the observation to another month.

Plans to support teams can take a variety of formats – and, as outlined previously, depending on the internal quality assurance model in the organisation, the information contained in it may be stored in more than one place and may be the responsibility of more than one person. However, it is important that it is documented, that a variety of support and development opportunities are open to team members, and ultimately that their need for support is met and as a result their practice improves.

Page 68 shows an example of one type of plan that can be effective in ensuring that support is organised and becomes a simple record kept of what actually took place. This is an annual plan that would be drawn up by the IQA, or maybe the IQAC. It is circulated and agreed with the tutors/assessors in the team and then accepted by senior staff. The detailed documents related to each of the activities (such as minutes or observation checklists) would be stored separately.

In the first instance, the owner of the document – in this case the IQAC – would produce a summary plan like this with no specific dates. The dates for the year will have been agreed towards the end of the previous year, so that each individual has all the dates related to them in their planners in advance. As the month of the activity approaches, the IQA will then confirm the actual dates with the team members.

As the year progresses, so the owner of the document – in this case the IQAC – will update the content on a monthly basis, and gradually it becomes a record of who has attended what activity. The plan below has been updated up to July.

As it becomes a record, it enables everyone to be aware of what support has been and is available throughout the year and what has been utilised by whom. For the IQAC it gives an overall picture of who attends what and can be very useful in identifying team members who regularly miss taking part in some or all agreed activities. The reasons for this can then be explored with the individuals concerned during routine one-to-one meetings.

The IQA support plan is a valuable tool in ensuring that team members have regular contact and are able to share concerns and issues, and it gives a structure for providing regular and routine support throughout a year.

Example of an IQAC/QAC Annual Support Plan 2011

IQAC: J Adebayo

Tutor/Assessor	Jan	Feb	March	April	May	June	July	Aug	Sept	Oct	Nov	Dec
A Beddington	TM OTO	OTO		TM & SA		OBS	TM	OTO		TM		SA
B Longford	TM	OTO		TM & SA			TM OBS	OBS	OTO OBS	TM		SA
C Styanovic	TM		OTO	TM & SA	OTO		TM	OBS	OBS	TM OTO		SA
D Powell	TM	OBS	OBS	TM & SA OTO			TM			TM	OTO	SA
E Smith	TM		OBS	TM & SA	OTO		TM			TM		SA OTO
F Achary	TM			TM & SA OBS	OBS	OTO	TM			TM		SA
G McAndrew	TM			TM & SA	OBS	OBS	TM OTO OBS	OTO		TM		SA

KEY

Abbreviation	Stands for
TM	Team Meeting – 1st Monday each quarter
OTO	One-to-one meeting
SA	Standardisation activity
OBS	Observation by IQA

Highlighted colour	Stands for
GREEN	Carried out as planned
BLUE	Delayed – new date set
YELLOW	Rearranged date – now done
RED	Not attended/completed

This does not mean that informal or 'on demand' support would not also be provided to tutors and assessors as issues arise. However, experience has shown that when regular support is available the need for informal and 'on demand' support does reduce. This has a knock-on effect, whereby the IQA or IQAC's time is less side-tracked into dealing with unanticipated and 'urgent' issues as the year progresses.

In addition, it provides a tool for demonstrating to internal departments (such as Human Resources and Health and Safety) and also to external agencies (including the AOs, inspectors and Health and Safety Executive) that tutors' and assessors' need for support is both recognised and being addressed by the activities being carried out.

'Consistency is contrary to nature, contrary to life. The only completely consistent people are dead.' Aldous Huxley

---

ACTIVITY

Can you suggest any additional ways in which an IQA could support their tutor or assessor team?

STANDARDISATION [6317 unit 401 AC4.2]

Consistency

Everyone in the learning process aims for standardisation and consistency in the way that programmes and qualifications are delivered and assessed. However, this is very much aspirational, and a process rather than a specific goal to be achieved, as both are extremely difficult to accomplish.

If it were possible to achieve total consistency in performance then football players would always perform at a high standard and the team would always behave in the same way. Team managers might wish for this and train teams with this aim in mind, but the performance on the pitch rarely conforms and is often totally different in each game.

So what the IQA *can* do is to control the variables that it is possible to control, and support and encourage everyone to approach tasks and activities in similar ways. Then the IQA monitors and tries to keep everyone on track … while trying not to stifle creativity and innovation. It's called 'a challenge'…!

A standardisation activity in relation to learning is something that the IQA organises for team members to provide an opportunity for them to:

- reach a common understanding about requirements
- share ideas
- look at each other's practice
- consider different approaches
- consider and compare their work with others'
- consider and compare the judgements made by others
- see how others complete documentation.

AOs insist on standardisation taking place to try to promote consistency in work and decision-making in centres delivering learning. It is important that if a person completes a programme of learning or a qualification anywhere in the UK, that they should have gone through similar processes as anyone else going through the same programme or qualification irrespective of where that learning took place. This is the 'big picture' aim of carrying out standardisation.

This is far more difficult to achieve than you might imagine – in fact, it may not be possible to achieve. There will be differences in how learning is delivered in response to the needs of learners, and some situations demand different approaches – so those delivering learning often approach it in very different ways. For example, the same programme or qualification can be delivered by face-to-face tuition or via distance learning materials with online support. It might be delivered to a group of learners or on a one-to-one basis. As a result it is not possible to achieve genuine uniformity across the country. Nor is this really desirable. It is, after all, important that local and even individual needs are met by the learning, so there will inevitably be differences in what, how, where and why learning is delivered.

However, what should not be different on any given programme or qualification is what the learners have learned, and it is necessary that all the requirements have been met and – where required – that the learning has been tested.

So an IQA is aiming to ensure that work carried out by their team is as consistent as possible, across learners, methods of assessment, types of evidence, record keeping and assessment sites.

ACTIVITY

Do you recall the acronym that ensures that IQAs cover all necessary factors in their sample planning? If you need to look it up, it is on page 41.

Standardisation can also help to ensure that:

- team members are consistent in their interpretation of the content and requirements contained within programmes and qualifications
- there is accuracy and consistency of assessment decisions between assessors
- tutors and assessors comply with the assessment strategy for the qualification they are assessing (if applicable).

A starting point

The process of standardisation should start as soon as new programme or qualification content is received. It is very useful if the IQA gets the team together and they work through the requirements point by point, agreeing what it is they are expecting to see in relation to each.

This might be in relation to what each unit/module should contain or what its outcome should be. So, for example, there might be a discussion about what a training session on Unit 1 might need to include, and then a discussion about what work the learner has to do to meet the requirements of testing in Unit 1.

If the IQA plans the development out well, much time can be saved by identifying units that are similar in style, content or requirements, and grouping these units together for the team to work on. Most IQAs would start by getting the team to look at any mandatory areas together and then look at the optional areas later.

Clearly this process does not have to be completed in one sitting, but can be done over a period of time as the programme progresses. However, unless it is carried out in a timely fashion it could mean that the team are only a few steps ahead of the learners on each unit/module.

On an ongoing basis, as we have seen on page 42, the IQA will carry out risk assessments that will include the programme and the team, and then produce a plan of what and when they will carry out the sample. Having got the team together to initially plan out the programme as described above, they may also plan an early standardisation activity. (This might be included as an additional activity on the IQAC's annual support plan.)

At this point it is common for a team to get together to standardise what they have done and any judgements they have made – for example, after the first module or unit has been completed. This gives them an opportunity to spend time together and reflect on how the first sessions or work have gone. It also allows them to review whether what they had originally thought was accurate, and to reach a common agreement about the content and assessment so far. They can then determine whether it is at the right level before any learners start on the next module or unit.

Yet another internal quality assurance tale…

An IQA was carrying out a thematic sample in a unit about leading meetings on a management qualification. She focused on the minutes of meetings that learners (managers) had presented as part of their products of work. She was surprised to find that two of the four assessors in her team were judging very poor-quality minutes to be acceptable and giving no action points related to them.

The other two assessors had recognised poor practice in their learners and given action points requiring that minutes in subsequent meetings should include who was present, the date and time of the meeting, actions arising from each point, the date of the next meeting, etc.

The IQA anonymised and copied the poor-quality minutes and handed them out at a standardisation meeting where all four assessors (working in pairs) vehemently asserted that they were very poor practice and they would have given action points related to improving them. The IQA asked them again in pairs to actually produce the feedback, justification and action points that they would have given to their learners had they assessed that evidence.

In the next one-to-one session with the assessors who had not given action points, the IQA used the actual assessment documents where no feedback had been given about the minutes and discussed what had happened and why they had not action-planned the learners. Both assessors said they had not really thought about the quality of the content of the evidence – they had just checked that minutes had been included in the evidence.

At the next standardisation activity, the IQA picked up on the issue of ensuring that assessors considered improving management practice with their learners, and all agreed that it was a useful reminder of their role in developing managers as well as assessing evidence.

The moral of the story is – good IQA practice can improve assessment and learner performance.

Talk to other organisations about activities they use to standardise.

Ongoing standardisation

As the programme or qualification progresses, the IQA will plan further standardisation activities – as can be seen on the annual support plan on page 68.

The nature of these activities will depend on the needs of the team members, the programme requirements, the amount of time available and what has been completed at that point. The IQA needs to plan the activities so that they take place when there has been sufficient work done on the programme or qualification to provide material for discussion. But they must not delay to a point where if any issues are found they cannot be rectified and remedial action would prove very difficult to successfully carry out.

In the table below are the types of activities that IQAs typically use to standardise in their teams.

Standardisation activity	What the activity entails
Working through requirements together and agreeing expected outcomes	Tutors, assessors and IQAs work through the contents of a unit and identify what they will need to deliver and how, what they would ask learners to do and what they would expect to see as a result (as described above).
Assessing each other's learners	IQA takes one unit from a candidate and gives it to another assessor, then the two assessors discuss the outcome.
The team watches a recorded activity and gives feedback	IQA records an activity that an assessor is assessing (such as something they are observing), then other assessors can view the recording and assess the activity themselves using the genuine documentation. Assessors can then compare their judgements and the feedback that they would have given the learners.
The team watches a recorded training session and gives feedback	IQA records a training session, other team members watch the recording, complete an observation checklist and give feedback to tutor.
Assessors judging evidence together	Assessors can examine work products together, judge the work, agree on an assessment decision and formulate feedback for the candidate.
Team members get together to agree on what the answers to questions should contain	Tutors and assessors can work together to agree what the answer to each question should contain. This activity is used to agree an outline of what should appear – not a model answer. The outline can then be used when assessing or marking future questions.
Team members observe each other working and give feedback	Individual team members can observe each other planning with learners, making assessment decisions and giving feedback to the learners. The observer can complete an IQA observation checklist and then use this to give feedback.

Final standardisation

Sometimes – particularly where the programme or qualification is being run for the first time – the IQA will plan a final standardisation. IQAs often carry this out by arranging a full review of the process involving everyone in the team. It can be done by gathering information electronically or by using a meeting. It enables the team to share and consider their experiences and should result in a common understanding of what happened on the programme. From this the IQA can produce a summative report, which is likely to include recommendations for future programmes.

The benefit of reviewing the programme face-to-face is that it provides an opportunity for:

- the IQA to give an overview of the total process
- everyone to share experiences
- all parties to discuss how the process has worked
- the entire team to focus in on any anomalies
- agreement about any changes for the future
- a future plan to be drawn up
- individual/team development needs to be identified.

The IQA may then produce a short report or paper summing up the reflections of the team, highlighting issues and recommending where changes can be made to improve consistency and quality. This type of report can be very useful to those who take part in the review, but can also serve as a mechanism for requesting additional or alternative resources for future programmes. In addition, it can be shown to the external quality assurer as an example of the centre's commitment to continuous improvement in their delivery of the programme or qualification.

Record everything!

RECORDING AND INFORMATION MANAGEMENT [6317 unit 401 AC5.1]

In previous sections we have talked a great deal about IQA procedures, planning and monitoring, and supporting the tutor and assessor team. In all of these activities there is a requirement for the IQA to keep adequate and detailed records of what has been planned, agreed, then carried out. These records may be required internally by colleagues, line managers and auditors, and externally by regulators, inspectors and by representatives of the AOs.

In addition to providing data to demonstrate IQA practice, the records are also essential as a mechanism for reflection, learning and ensuring that the team does not repeat mistakes in the future.

These records can take many forms – and they can be electronic or on paper. Whatever method of storage is used, the most important consideration is that they are always readily available when requested, are held securely where necessary and are kept up to date.

They can also serve many purposes – in previous sections we saw internal quality assurance plans turning into records, and in the Appendices are a range of documents that can be used to record observations, etc, carried out by the IQA (see Appendices 5, 6, 7 and 8).

These are some of the records that IQAs typically maintain:

Type of record	What it might contain
Internal quality assurance strategy:	• copy of original strategy • updated versions • related documents.
Annual quality development plan:	• a current plan for what activities take place during the year – and when (if relevant).
Team member records. Each person's records should contain:	• CPD plans for individual team members • CPD records • CVs • copies of relevant certificates • annual TNAs or skillscans • all written feedback from IQA • record of one-to-one support meetings • other performance-related documents.
IQA sample plans and records, such as:	• all sample plans related to each programme or qualification • related rationales (if required) • copies of records of sampling undertaken • copies of feedback from IQA to tutor/assessor.
Related to requirements of AO, for example:	• organisational chart • correspondence with awarding organisation • approval documents • last EQA reports • updates • registration and certification claims (in small centres) • Equal Opportunities and Diversity monitoring • Health and Safety records.
Sets of standards, including:	• a set of the requirements/qualification handbook for each programme or qualification being offered.
Meetings/standardisation records, such as:	• annual plan of meetings • agendas • sets of minutes/notes from the meetings.

Type of record	What it might contain
Support plan for team:	• copy of the original support plan • copies of updated ones.
Master set of documents:	• all the current versions of regularly used documents in the centre.

One of the most important features of IQA records is that they are sufficiently detailed and up to date so that the IQA can show anyone what has been done and demonstrate that it has been carried out in a thorough way. This is often one of the areas of IQA work that EQAs find requires further development.

In many centres, the level of detail recorded is scant, and so it is difficult for anyone who did not take part in the activity to properly understand what has taken place and why. As a result the IQA is unable to prove the quality or depth of what they have done – though they may be able to show the outcome. An example of this is when an IQA carries out a full standardisation activity and then only records that it happened in one line on the minutes of the meeting where it took place.

As with many records, IQA records should be completed with sufficient detail for a third party to be able to read them, pick up the thread of what took place and be in a position to understand enough to progress the activity.

It is also important that the IQA makes sense of what has been found in any given period and interprets this information for other team members and decision makers both within the organisation and externally. This might involve the IQA producing reports on a variety of areas, such as trends in assessment practice, and providing both quantitative and qualitative data as required.

ACTIVITY

What kinds of:
1 Quantitative data do you think the IQA might collect?
2 Qualitative information do you think the IQA could produce?

The quantitative data that the IQA can gather is relatively straightforward – it often consists of information like an analysis of learner involvement, including:

- registrations
- attendance
- retention
- achievement
- progression to further qualifications
- complaints or appeals
- malpractice, eg plagiarism
- suspensions from programmes
- removal from programmes prior to completion.

The qualitative information is more complex and might include summaries or analysis of:
- workload issues
- trends picked up by the IQA
- recurring issues identified by the IQA
- learner evaluations
- Equal Opportunities monitoring
- why learners are slow to complete
- why learners fail to complete
- areas for development – of programmes and of team members.

Please see Appendices 11, 12 and 13 for examples of what different types of IQA reports might contain.

THE IQA'S ROLE IN DISPUTES AND APPEALS [6317 unit 401 AC4.3]

Although for many IQAs this will never happen during their career, as the person who is responsible for a team of tutors and/or assessors the IQA is inevitably the first point of contact when any disputes or appeals occur in a centre.

Each centre must have a policy that outlines for staff and learners the process to follow if a dispute, grievance or appeal should arise. These are also sometimes included in an organisation's overall policies.

Always get support from specialist colleagues (such as HR professionals) at the very start of managing a dispute, grievance or appeal.

ACTIVITY

In terms of internal quality assurance, briefly outline what you think each of the following means:
- dispute
- grievance
- appeal.

In the main, in relation to internal quality assurance:

- A **dispute** is where two or more parties cannot agree on something. This may be about one or more courses of action, behaviour, conduct or decisions taken. In a centre it could occur between members of the team or indeed between a team member and a learner.
- A **grievance** is often a complaint that is made when someone is unhappy with the work or behaviour of another person. In a centre the complaint may be made by a team member against a colleague or by a learner about a team member.
- An **appeal** would take place in a centre if a learner formally disagreed with an assessment or IQA decision related to their work.

As outlined above, centres must have procedures for handling disputes, grievances and appeals. An example of an appeals procedure can be found in Appendix 15. This gives an outline of the areas that should be included.

If a dispute, grievance or appeal takes place in a centre – as long as it does not relate to the IQA – then the first response is usually carried out by the IQA. However, as can be seen on page 79, the IQA will always need to work and administer programmes within the framework of the organisation's procedures and policies. In the event of a dispute, grievance or appeal, it is likely that the IQA would discuss the issue first with their line manager and then with the organisation's Human Resources (HR) department. In most organisations the HR policies would need to be followed and the centre's dispute, grievance or appeal procedures would be part of or in line with them.

The process for managing disputes and grievances is usually specifically outlined in an organisation's HR procedures. As a result these are not considered in any detail in this book.

However, in most organisations, the HR procedures would not include the type of appeals procedure required in a centre that is delivering accredited programmes and/or qualifications.

Therefore one of the IQA's very first tasks is often to write an appeal procedure that is in line with the AO requirements and does not impact on other HR procedures in the organisation. Appeals procedures can vary in format and content, though they often tend to be variations on a theme (for typical content see Appendix 15).

This procedure may need to be agreed with a variety of people – including the organisation's HR team – as it must not conflict or interfere with other procedures and practices already in existence. It is then distributed to team members and learners as part of an overall set of procedures or indeed as part of a Learner or Staff Handbook.

It is important that the content of the procedure is described to learners and new team members during their induction phase so that they are aware of their rights from the very start of their programme or work.

In the unlikely event of an appeal being raised, the first action taken by the IQA is to record the appeal on an appeals log. Every centre should have an appeals log so that they can quickly demonstrate to anyone what appeals the centre has had and how they have been managed. This appeals log should be maintained in the centre records (see Appendix 14 for the layout of a typical appeals log).

In essence the process of an appeal typically (but not definitively) looks something like this:

In an appeals procedure...

The learner discusses their concern about the assessment decision with the assessor who made it. Often this is sufficient to resolve any misunderstandings or errors that have occurred in the process.

However, in some cases it is not possible for the assessor and the learner to come to an agreement, or the assessor is unable to get the learner to understand and accept the decision. In this situation the assessor will refer the learner back to the IQA. This referral then triggers:

Stage One

This tends to be a verbal exploration of what has happened between the learner and the IQA, where an attempt is made to resolve the appeal amicably. If this is possible then the IQA will inform both parties in writing of the outcome and record what took place and how it has been resolved. They will also inform the EQA of the process and outcome.

If it is not possible to resolve the issue, the IQA will move the process on to a more formal footing.

Stage Two

The IQA may contact the EQA to give a view on the issue – particularly if the disagreement involves a technicality related to the programme or qualification. If the EQA is able to guide the centre to a resolution then the IQA will inform both parties in writing of the outcome and record what took place and how it has been resolved.

If the issue has not been resolved, the IQA will move the process to the final stage.

Stage Three

The IQA will carry out a full investigation into the issue and produce a report. This report will be considered by an appeals panel, which is likely to hold a 'hearing' where all parties will have an opportunity to put forward their point of view.

The appeals panel usually consists of the IQA, the organisation's HR manager, and an objective third party – possibly from another department, section or faculty to that where the appeal has arisen. It is possible that the EQA could be invited to be part of the panel. Whether they take part would be determined by the AO and may result in a cost to the organisation. When the hearing has listened to the opinions of everyone involved, the panel will then usually deliberate and take a decision that will be conveyed in writing. In most centres the decision of the appeals panel is deemed to be final.

Whatever stage the appeal reaches before resolution, it is usual that the IQA co-ordinates the entire process, and they are generally responsible for logging the appeal, maintaining related records, keeping the awarding organisation informed, organising the hearing and communicating the outcome to appropriate parties.

As mentioned in the start of this section, most IQAs never experience an appeal, as any problems are resolved informally and amicably and never progress to being a formal issue.

However, if a formal appeals process does take place, it is usually the IQA who:

- co-ordinates the process
- takes responsibility for progressing it to where a resolution can be reached
- maintains communication between all parties
- keeps records of what took place and the outcome.

Therefore it is important that IQAs feel confident in using the appeals process and fully understand the procedures they may have to implement.

It is also useful if they have undergone some conflict management, dispute resolution or mediation training in order to be able to resolve disputes, grievances and appeals at the least formal level and as amicably as possible.

In addition, it is important that when undertaking an appeal the IQAs feel – and indeed are – supported by other people in the organisation.

LEGAL ISSUES, POLICIES AND PROCEDURES [6317 unit 401 AC6.1 & 6.4]

LEGAL ISSUES

As you might imagine – given what has been outlined in previous sections – there are many areas of legislation that have an impact on internal quality assurance.

www.direct.gov.uk provides a series of useful summaries and explanations of the practical implications of all types of legislation. For example, in relation to the Data Protection Act, the information includes the following summary:

> **'Protecting your information**
> The Data Protection Act's rules are quite complex, but at the heart of it are eight common sense rules known as the "data protection principles".
>
> These principles require any organisation, corporation or governmental body that collects personal information to handle it safely. Anyone collecting personal information must:
> - fairly and lawfully process it
> - process it only for limited, specifically stated purposes
> - use the information in a way that is adequate, relevant and not excessive
> - use the information accurately
> - keep the information on file no longer than absolutely necessary
> - process the information in accordance with your legal rights
> - keep the information secure
> - never transfer the information outside the UK without adequate protection.
>
> All organisations collecting and using personal information are legally required to comply with these principles.
>
> The law provides stronger protection for more sensitive information – such as your ethnic background, political opinions, religious beliefs, health, sexual life or any criminal history...'

This is by far the clearest summary of the practical application of the Act that the author has seen to date. If you are an active IQA you might find it useful to familiarise yourself with the legislation to be sure that you do not inadvertently breach it.

ACTIVITY

Visit www.direct.gov.uk and look at the summaries of the following areas of legislation – all of which may impact on the role of an IQA:
1   Health and Safety
2   Employment
3   Data Protection and Confidentiality
4   Equality and Diversity
5   Age Discrimination

Having looked at the salient points of the relevant areas, how do you think they might affect the IQA in their day-to-day work? Which areas do you think would be of particular risk?

If you are already working as an IQA, check yourself against the summary points in the main pieces of legislation and think about changes you may need to introduce into your working practices.

Note here actions you could take in your work to ensure that you and your team do not contravene the legislation and to enable you to actively promote best practice.

1

2

3

4

5

POLICIES AND PROCEDURES

There are also a range of policies and procedures that IQAs are required to develop in some cases and comply with in their work.

Some are directly related to IQA practice (like the need to have a method of annually checking that team members continue to meet the requirements of the programme or qualification or the appropriate assessment strategy) and have to be clearly followed at all times.

Other policies or procedures have a more indirect impact. This could be where the 'approved centre' delivering the learning may only be a small part of a much larger organisation. An example of this could be (as mentioned in previous section) where a local authority has a centre but its HR policies apply to the entire workforce – including those employed in the approved centre. In this situation the IQA may have to comply with them and, for example, use the authority's disciplinary procedure when addressing performance issues with a member of the tutoring or assessment team. IQAs sometimes find that these policies are not suitable for their purposes but they have no choice but to use them.

What policies and procedures already in place in your organisation could/do impact on your IQA role?

When you have identified them, it might be useful to talk to the professionals in your organisation who are responsible for their overall implementation – such as your HR department or Health and Safety team. They can be a valuable source of guidance to an IQA.

There may be a range of work practices or organisational policies that have an effect on an IQA. Here are some of the most common ones:

Appeals
Most organisations have procedures entitling employees to appeal against decisions taken about them in the workplace. These procedures will apply to employed tutors and assessors, and so it is possible that they could be invoked if a tutor or assessor disagreed with actions taken or feedback given by an IQA.

Appraisal
IQAs often take part in – or even solely conduct – the performance appraisals of the tutors and/or assessors who report to them. This will require them to use HR procedures that may or may not be appropriate to the specific roles they are appraising and the relationship that they have with their team members. Often the IQA–tutor or IQA–assessor relationship is less formal and operates more on the level of colleague than the line manager role that exists elsewhere in organisations.

Codes of practice
Many organisations have specific codes of practice for their employees. These may cover areas such as dress codes, acceptable behaviour, punctuality, etc. These too will have an impact on what the IQA may have to monitor as part of their work.

However, there are also codes of practice related to the roles of professionals in the field of learning. These may include general areas such as professional behaviour, personal and professional integrity, declaring conflicts of interest, etc, or they may be specifically related to the field that the IQA works in. For example, if the IQA works in the Health and Social Care sector there will be additional, specific codes of practice for the sector that must be adhered to by the IQA and all members of the tutor and assessor team.

The IfL launched a Code of Practice for learning professionals in 2008 that may be of interest to IQAs. It can be found at www.ifl.ac.uk.

Confidentiality

Many organisations have confidentiality clauses in their contracts of employment or in contracts with self-employed workers. Therefore all members of the team should be aware of the need to not disclose information about anyone – but particularly in relation to details referring to colleagues or learners.

In addition, it may be required that the IQA keeps the learner's employer, or the funding organisation informed of their progress. IQAs sometimes find that passing on information like this raises issues. To avoid difficulties in this area it is important that staff members and learners in particular are informed in advance that information – for example, about learner progress – may be shared with other people, including their employing organisation.

Discipline/capability

If an IQA has an under-performing team member, managing their performance inevitably requires the use of organisational HR procedures – which again may or may not be appropriate to the situation.

Equality and Diversity

The organisation may have specific policies and procedures promoting good practice in relation to issues of equality and diversity. These might include ensuring that the people who work in the team reflect the mix of people in the local population and are representative of its ethnic, cultural and linguistic make-up. The IQA will need to ensure that their actions do not contravene these policies – and in fact actively promote good practice.

Health and Safety

The organisation may have specific policies and procedures related to working practices that have a different application in the roles of tutor/assessor. For example, the organisation may have a Lone Worker Policy for specific job roles within the organisation. However, depending on the content, a policy like this may impact directly on a peripatetic assessor's ability to carry out their role, and may therefore require the IQA to interpret the policy into a set of working practices or guidelines that can assist and not impede or even restrict the assessor. In addition, peripatetic assessors often do not fit the profile of what is considered to be a Lone Worker and can be overlooked in any risk assessment of lone working.

A salutary tale of Lone Worker safety

A peripatetic hairdressing assessor was also responsible for visiting potential new salons in which to place young people for work experience so that they could undertake hairdressing qualifications. Once they were settled on the placement, she then visited the young people on a weekly basis to action plan them on their qualification and give support to both the learners and the staff training and assessing them.

She had identified that a new salon had opened on a quiet side street in one of the local towns and she made an appointment to meet the owner there at 4pm one afternoon in November. They got on famously and she ended up staying until 6pm discussing what the salon could offer, requirements for the learners to attend sessions covering knowledge requirements, how they could support the salon staff, what workplace assessment would mean to them, etc.

She had noticed that during their meeting the owner was moving closer to her and that he seemed to be becoming increasingly over-familiar. As the meeting was drawing to a close, they left the office and moved downstairs and she realised that the salon was empty and closed to the public, it was dark, staff had gone home and other than the two of them there was no one else in the building or in the street outside.

She felt very uncomfortable and uneasy and made ready to leave, whereupon the salon owner barred her exit and in a joking but insistent way said she should stay and celebrate the start of their working relationship by having a drink with him. She didn't want to lose the placement, nor for him to think that she felt intimidated, so she agreed to have a small glass of wine then – also in a joking manner – she threatened to call the police unless he let her go. After they finished their drink he tried to coax her to stay but she was insistent. He was not very happy but he did let her leave without any further difficulty.

When she told her IQA the story the following day, they identified that their organisation had a Lone Worker Policy that had never been applied in relation to peripatetic assessors as they were not really perceived to be working alone. In addition, no risk assessment had been done on their role.

(Incidentally, the organisation decided not to use the salon to train young people and did not send other team members there.)

Having reflected on what had happened, the IQA interpreted the content of the Lone Worker Policy and wrote a set of practical guidelines for peripatetic assessors. These were implemented, introducing simple procedures such as:
- appointments to visit employer premises were planned for the morning wherever possible, but always had to be booked to take place before 3pm

- if the location was remote or it was clear that there would be no one else at the venue at any point, then wherever possible the person would be invited to attend the centre premises rather than the assessor going to them
- an itinerary system was set up so an office-based staff member knew where assessors were working and roughly what time they were supposed to complete the visit, reach home or be back at the office
- assessors working away from base phoned the office when they had finished for the day.

This is just one example of an existing Health and Safety procedure that could have helped the IQA to protect their peripatetic assessor – but it had not been implemented as it was not perceived to be relevant to or to be pertinent to the role.

Progression

For example, moving a promising tutor or assessor into an IQA role may not be straightforward. It might be viewed as a promotion and require a change of status, salary scale and working terms and conditions. These things are all functions managed by HR – often with set procedures to be followed.

Recruitment

IQAs often have to comply with HR procedures when recruiting people to their team. This can be tricky in some situations – for example, where the organisation is trying to redeploy people who the IQA does not feel are suitable to the team – even though they may be able to meet the requirements.

Security and access to data

Many centres have very strict guidelines about access to information. This is especially important in situations where the information may contain or be stored in close proximity to sensitive data such as names, addresses and employment history. The IQA will need to organise their systems and information to complement or at least not contravene these guidelines. They will particularly need to be sure that their team maintains good practice and security when materials have to be transported outside the main base. It is while being transported or transmitted that the greatest risk to information security occurs.

ACTIVITY

Outline how information is stored securely in your organisation. If your organisation has a communication policy, consider how the storage, security, transmission and accessibility of learner information in your centre fit into this policy.

Staff development

Identifying that a tutor or assessor needs further development might involve an IQA in negotiating additional study leave, or resources for their team member with the HR department or the person's line manager (if the IQA is not in this role).

REFLECTIVE PRACTICE AND CPD

[6317 unit 401 AC6.3]

REFLECTIVE PRACTICE

Encourage your team to reflect at every meeting.

In all professional practice and in all roles where responsibility is held in learning organisations, there is a requirement for people to reflect on their decisions, actions and the resultant outcomes. They need to consider what they have done, identify if there were alternative courses of action that might have been more effective and learn from the experiences that they have had. In addition, when involved in learning programmes there is an opportunity to role model this as good practice to other team members and learners.

ACTIVITY

Think about a piece of work or a task that you have recently carried out that involved you working with other people or leading their work. Think about it in detail, if possible break it down into steps and be brutally honest with yourself!

Consider:
- what went well
- what did not go to plan
- what you would do differently if you were required to do it again
- what you learned from the experience
- what you can do to improve your performance.

These sorts of questions are the basis of reflective practice – they work well for IQAs. They can be applied to everyday occurrences in the workplace, specific tasks undertaken and one-off projects. They can also – if adapted slightly – be used when reflecting on learning activities in general.

Reflective practice is said to be a process of considering or analysing experiences in order to learn from them, and is very much a feature of the principle of 'lifelong learning'. There are a wide range of models of reflection readily available on the internet. However, most follow the same overriding principle – that it is a useful activity which promotes learning and can result in improvements in professional practice.

ACTIVITY

Look up at least three different models of reflection. Which one(s) best fits your style of reflective practice?

It is important that IQAs lead the way in implementing good practice with team members. So it is expected that IQAs at all times behave with integrity and professionalism, and demonstrate sound practice in all aspects of their work. This applies in equal measure to reflective practice.

An IQA should be regularly reflecting on their work, on experiences they have had, on learning activities and on information that they have gathered. By so doing they should be in a good position to improve their practice and develop the quality of their work. But they can also then encourage team members to reflect on their own experiences and look to learn from everything that they encounter in their tutor and/or assessor work.

ACTIVITY

A very good starting point for reflecting on your performance as an IQA is to have a dispassionate look at yourself and itemise where (in your IQA role) your Strengths, Weaknesses, Opportunities and Threats (SWOT) lie.
You could start by completing something like this:

Strengths as an IQA
1
2
3
4

Weaknesses as an IQA
1
2
3
4

Opportunities in your role
1
2
3
4

Threats to your role
1
2
3
4

(You could of course adapt this form and use it with your tutors and/or assessors in their roles. They could also utilise it with learners.)

The IQA could then use the outcome of such an analysis to identify their development needs and clarify possible areas where they need to change their practice. These would be recorded on a development or CPD plan (see Appendix 16) for the forthcoming period. The outcome of the SWOT analysis could also be used to form the basis of a discussion with someone who may be able to give feedback and possibly put forward their opinion about what the analysis appears to indicate.

FEEDBACK AND REFLECTION

In addition to reflective practice, informal feedback from others can be extremely useful, whether they are colleagues, peers, line managers, mentors or learners. This feedback can provide information and opinions that may assist the IQA in considering areas where they need to develop skills, knowledge and understanding. These could then be recorded on the development or CPD plan.

Also sharing a reflection on an experience and requesting feedback from a trusted source can allow an IQA to explore difficult situations and might result in significant changes to the way that they approach such issues in the future.

Informal feedback can provide perspectives that may change an IQA's approach or working practices and so improve their ability to carry out the role.

In most organisations, in addition to informal feedback there would also be a range of formal opportunities for the IQA to gain feedback. For example, they or their work will be:
- observed by their EQA
- sampled by their EQA
- included in the content of EQA reports
- monitored or supervised by a line manager or Lead IQA (where such a role exists)
- the subject of the organisation's performance review or appraisal process.

This type of feedback would usually be infrequent, and given in relation to an agreed set of criteria or objectives against which the person's work or performance had been 'judged'. Inevitably, then, the feedback is likely to relate only to the criteria or objectives and is usually given in a formal way. This can obviously be useful but is perhaps not the most effective type of feedback for the IQA who is looking to be a regular reflective practitioner.

Many organisations have a 'buddying' or mentorship programme that provides a framework for feedback to be given in a non-threatening and supportive way. It is far easier to discuss sensitive issues and possible mistakes of judgement or action with an objective third party than it is with someone involved in the process or who knows others who are involved. This process can then provide regular opportunities for the IQA to verbally reflect or consider issues and experiences and then have feedback that is more informal in nature and content. It is particularly useful for new or newly qualified IQAs.

CONTINUING PROFESSIONAL DEVELOPMENT
[6317 unit 401 AC6.3]

For IQAs there is often a need to carry out at least two types of CPD every year. They will need to keep their IQA practice up to date, but they may also need to maintain the currency of their technical knowledge related to the qualifications or programmes for which they are responsible. In addition, in some sectors the IQA has to be a current assessor in their field – sometimes by both continuing to practise as an assessor and maintaining their CPD in this role too. This does, however, differ from sector to sector.

Before an IQA takes any action on CPD, it is wise to check the assessment guidance or strategy for any programmes or qualifications that they are going to be working with, as they may contain specific CPD requirements and evidence on an annual basis.

As outlined above, an IQA would usually have an annual development or CPD plan (see Appendix 16) that they follow – this could arise from the requirements of the strategy, or from other activities, such as a TNA, SWOT analysis, performance appraisal or other form of activity designed to identify development needs.

If relevant, look at the assessment strategy or guidance provided in support of the programmes or qualifications that you will be working with. What CPD requirements will you will need to meet each year?

CPD activities can take many forms, and – again, in an effort to model good practice – IQAs should try to utilise a range of these in any given year (as long as they are acceptable in relation to any specifications they need to meet). Here are some of the main activities that IQAs might engage in:

- requesting feedback
- undertaking training courses
- individual research
- attending forums
- completing related qualifications
- shadowing another IQA
- training as an EQA
- standardisation activities
- undertaking related reading
- attending relevant meetings or conferences
- being observed.

There are a wide range of tools available for storing CPD information – both electronic and on paper. A very important feature, however, is that this process should not be complicated and records should be easy to maintain. See Appendix 17 for an example of what a simple document for recording CPD could contain.

In addition, some professional institutes have their own facilities for storing CPD records online.

Whatever form the processes of reflection, analysis, development planning and recording take, the focus for the IQA must always be on how this can:

- meet any stated requirements
- improve quality
- enhance professional practice
- increase efficiency and effectiveness.

'Almost all quality improvement comes via simplification of design, manufacturing... layout, processes, and procedures.'
Tom Peters, American businessman

SUMMARY:

The following points were covered in Part 2: Internal quality assurance:

- models of internal quality assurance in the UK
- the main functions of internal quality assurance
- roles and responsibilities in the quality assurance team
- how internal quality assurance is carried out
- documenting, planning and implementing an internal quality assurance system
- planning, supporting and evaluating learning delivery and assessment
- sampling
- supporting tutor and assessor performance
- making decisions – judging quality
- feedback
- standardisation
- recording and information management
- the IQA's role in disputes and appeals
- legal issues, policies and procedures
- reflective practice and CPD.

PART 3: EXTERNAL QUALITY ASSURANCE

What are the functions and roles involved in external quality assurance? How should you tackle planning, sampling, evaluating quality, giving feedback and being a reflective practitioner?

'A failure will not appear until a unit has passed final inspection.'
Arthur Bloch

WHAT IS EXTERNAL QUALITY ASSURANCE?

As mentioned in Part 2: Internal quality assurance, the national regulators (see page 15) require that AOs have mechanisms in place to organise the approval and regular monitoring of the organisations that become their 'approved centres'. They do this by using a process commonly referred to as external quality assurance. The AO will select representatives who are often technical experts in their field to carry out support and monitoring of the centres. The AO then provides policies, procedures and a structure or framework for the representatives to work effectively and consistently. External quality assurance takes place in relation to accredited programmes and qualifications across the UK and internationally, and is part of the national picture – or overall framework – of monitoring, developing and improving learning provision.

There are a range of reasons why external quality assurance is necessary and is a mandatory requirement of AOs operating in the UK system of vocational learning:

- The government funds much of the vocational learning delivered in the UK. This comes with an understandable need to monitor value for money. This value is generally measured in terms of what is being delivered and what is being achieved.
- The funding bodies have neither the capacity nor the expertise to carry out the activities themselves, so they work closely with the regulators (see page 15) to ensure value for money.
- The regulators monitor and evaluate the organisations who have the access to the technical expertise to carry out suitable checks, ie the AOs.
- AOs need a mechanism to establish that the organisations who are going to deliver the qualifications can meet the basic requirements for carrying this out. They begin to monitor whether an organisation is in a position to deliver their programmes or qualifications by using an approval process, where centres have to demonstrate that they are 'fit' organisations and able to meet the requirements, eg that they have suitable resources, people, systems, etc.
- Thereafter, AOs need to have a way of monitoring that the organisational requirements continue to be met year on year across all qualifications delivered. *This is the main function of external quality assurance.*
- AOs also need to confirm that the technical requirements of their qualifications continue to be met. *This is why EQAs are usually experienced practitioners in particular sectors and recognised as 'experts' in their field.*

- AOs need a mechanism for ensuring that the integrity of the qualifications being delivered in their name is maintained.
- AOs must have a way of evaluating the learner's experience while undertaking their qualifications.

THE MOST COMMON MODEL OF EXTERNAL QUALITY ASSURANCE

In Part 2 this was illustrated by the model on page 22 showing the reporting structure common in many centres.

There are a number of ways of externally assuring the quality of a learning programme or qualification. These start with specifying what a centre needs to have in place, and requirements that it has to meet, in order to be allowed or 'approved' to deliver the programme or qualification. The process carries on through to the ongoing monitoring of these requirements to ensure that they continue to be met and quality is maintained – and, wherever possible, improved.

THE FOCUS OF EXTERNAL QUALITY ASSURANCE

The monitoring of quality can be carried out using a number of methods and utilising the skills of the AO representatives in a variety of ways. How it is implemented will largely depend on what is perceived to be its purpose. Between 1990 and 2009, this purpose was generally said to be 'policing the standards'. In other words, EQAs (or External Verifiers, as they were then known) acted as inspectors who checked that centres complied with the NOS on which the programmes and qualifications were largely based.

From 2006 onwards there has been a move in the UK towards devolving the responsibility for quality assurance down to centres, with the regulators applying a 'lighter touch' in their monitoring. Consequently this has provided an opportunity for AOs to change and diversify how they monitor quality.

Since 2009, the purpose of external quality assurance has become focused more on supporting, guiding and developing organisations and their people, to enable them to be good at what they do and to deliver a quality service to learners.

With the introduction of the Qualification Credit Framework (QCF) in 2010 and 2011, there has been a perceptible change in the way that external quality assurance is carried out by all AOs.

The change is towards guidance and support of centres at the earliest stages, to assist them to 'get it right' rather than focusing effort on finding out further along in the process what it had gone wrong. As a number of centres regularly said to their External Verifiers, 'Tell us what we should be doing – don't just come and tell us when we haven't done it!'

This approach has a high number of benefits because it is:
- less punitive
- focused on developing quality
- more conciliatory
- increasingly developmental in tone
- more supportive
- positive
- less hierarchical
- more flexible.

This change of emphasis has enabled AOs to revise how they organise the external quality assurance that they deliver.

For example, when many centres were delivering National Vocational Qualifications (NVQs) there was a regulatory requirement to carry out an External Verification Activity twice every year. There were strict guidelines to be followed in how this was to be carried out and what the outcomes could be.

With the emergence of the QCF came a lighter touch and less specific requirements – AOs were able to put in place a more tailored series of support and monitoring activities that can be adapted and designed to meet the specific needs of a centre, its delivery team and its learners.

These support activities might still be a visit from a technical expert EQA, but alternatively they could be anything from a range of activities such as:
- an advisory visit to assist a team to fully understand the requirements of a qualification
- carrying out a standardisation activity with a centre team
- centre team members attending training
- a systems audit focusing on the quality of the internal systems the centre uses.

THE MAIN FUNCTIONS OF EXTERNAL QUALITY ASSURANCE [6312 unit 404 AC1.1]

As we have seen, there are a large number of diverse reasons why quality assurance is mandatory on accredited programmes and qualifications in the UK.

It is the local application of a national requirement that AOs approve, monitor and review that organisations delivering accredited programmes and qualifications meet the requirements and maintain and improve quality on an ongoing basis. External quality assurance is how AOs achieve this.

In order to ensure that they are able to approve and monitor the technical content of what is being delivered, AOs usually select people who are recognised as having considerable technical expertise in the sector to carry out the approval process and ongoing monitoring of their centres (see page 107 for details of EQA recruitment).

External quality assurance models and requirements may differ a great deal between AOs.

However, the people selected also have to be aware of the importance of other factors, such as structures, systems, risk management and integrity, in order to be able to fully carry out the role. This is because external quality assurance is about more than just being sure that a centre has the technical expertise to deliver a programme or qualification.

The main functions of external quality assurance are:

Assessing and managing risk
EQAs make plans and judgements based on risk analysis and then help centres to manage that risk.

Checking compliance
EQAs must be sure that regulatory and AO stated requirements are met and agree action if they are not.

Communication with centres
The EQA needs to keep a two-way channel of information open between the AO and the centre. As the AO representative, the EQA is able to communicate information from the AO to centres and contextualise it so that they better understand how it relates to them and their circumstances. In addition, for many centres the EQA is their main source of information from the AO about future developments and forthcoming changes.

Ensuring accuracy and consistency

This is done by monitoring assessment/marking across assessors, sites, learners and IQAs to promote as much consistent practice as is feasible.

Evaluating quality

This is necessary to establish that requirements are met and to suggest ways to improve practice.

Identifying issues and trends

EQAs are well placed to identify issues and underlying trends, eg in assessment practice, about which the AO can then provide additional guidance.

Imposing control

The external quality assurance process is the main way in which AOs maintain a measure of control over how their centres deliver the accredited programmes or qualifications.

Monitoring internal quality assurance practice

The EQA must ensure that internal quality assurance has a sound rationale, is planned, thorough, takes place at suitable points, identifies important issues, supports tutors and assessors, etc.

Record keeping

The EQA must ensure that the AO has accurate records of what has been found or reported in the sampling, and develop centres to maintain accurate and detailed records of their processes and practice.

Supporting and developing centre staff

The EQA assists teams to carry out their roles well and to identify areas where they could adapt or improve their practice.

Taking decisions and making recommendations

The EQA takes decisions based on what they find or are told by a centre. They give the centre feedback to assist them to develop their services. EQAs then make recommendations to the AO as to how the centre can/should progress.

Upholding integrity

This ensures that processes are transparent and robust, requirements have been met, the specified conditions have been maintained and that the integrity of the programme or qualification has not been compromised.

All of these functions are explored in more detail in the following sections.

In addition, external quality assurance gives a further measure of objectivity, as the EQA is not a member of the team at the centre but is an unrelated 'fresh pair of eyes' who can often see clearly areas for development that people who work within the centre perhaps cannot identify.

EQAs also have a huge advantage over staff working in centres as they are involved in monitoring programmes and qualifications in a range of organisations and will have valuable insights and ideas that they can disseminate to others. Therefore, since 2009, they have become more often viewed as a resource rather than an 'inspector'.

THE ROLE OF THE EQA [6312 unit 404 AC1.3]

As a starting point it is useful to keep in mind that the EQA role has many similarities to the IQA role – but that it is carried out on a 'one step removed' basis. So the EQA will undertake many activities that are similar to those of the IQA, but from an external standpoint. The main areas of similarity are outlined in the table below.

EQA has to...	IQA has to...
Maintain contact and good communication with centres	Maintain contact and good communication within the centre
Follow a set of external quality assurance procedures and processes provided by the AO	Follow the internal quality assurance policies and procedures for the team/centre
Use the rationale for sampling provided by the AO – such as CAMERA (see page 41)	Use the rationale for sampling in the centre – such as CAMERA (see page 41)
Risk assess centres, programmes and/or qualification routes	Risk assess teams, programmes and/or qualifications
Ensure that centres interpret, understand and apply the standards and requirements of the programmes and qualifications	Ensure that team members interpret, understand and apply the standards and requirements of the programmes and qualifications
Provide advice, guidance, information and support to centres	Provide advice, guidance, information and support to team members
Sample plan for a programme, qualification or set of qualifications	Sample plan for a programme, qualification, set of qualifications or cohort of learners
Monitor across programme/qualification routes and possibly across this and other centres	Monitor across programmes, qualifications and teams
Support, guide and advise centre teams	Support, guide and advise programme or qualification teams

EQA has to...	IQA has to...
Standardise across programme/qualification routes, the centre and possibly the wider qualification delivery across the UK	Standardise across programme/qualification routes and possibly across the centre
Monitor learning delivery, assessment and IQA practice	Monitor learning delivery and assessment practice
Evaluate staff (including IQA) skills, abilities, knowledge and competence to meet the requirements of the programme/qualification	Evaluate staff skills, abilities, knowledge and competence to meet the requirements of the programme/qualification
Hold discussions with IQAs, team members, learners and possibly others involved in the process, such as employers or witnesses	Hold discussions with team members, learners and others involved in the process, such as employers or witnesses
Observe learning delivery, assessment and IQA practice	Observe learning delivery and assessment practice
Record in detail the monitoring process, the external quality assurance decisions they have taken and the justifications for these decisions	Record in detail the monitoring process, the internal quality assurance decisions they have taken and the justifications for these decisions
Review centre and programme/qualification developments and progress	Review programme/qualification developments and progress
Take part in relevant CPD	Take part in relevant CPD

So there are many similarities between the roles, and most EQAs have previous experience in an IQA role. However, the major difference is that the EQA relies on someone else – the IQA – to carry out thorough monitoring on an ongoing basis, whereas the EQA has very limited opportunity to scrutinise what the centre is doing and can only take a 'snapshot' of the situation.

So the EQA needs to be able to follow the IQA audit trail and clearly see what has been sampled, found and acted upon by the IQA. If the IQA has carried out their role in full, this will give the EQA confidence that what they find in *their* 'snapshot' sample is representative of how the centre delivers and manages the programmes every day. This confidence then translates into less scrutiny by the EQA in the following period.

If you are an IQA but not an EQA, you might find it useful to keep in mind the similarities between the roles of IQA and EQA when continuing to read this part, as the role of EQA will be easier to envisage as a result.

QUALITIES, SKILLS AND ABILITIES NEEDED BY AN EQA

For anyone thinking about becoming an EQA, there are a number of aspects of the role that they should consider before making the application. Some of the qualities, skills and abilities required are listed below and it is likely that they would be outlined in some form of contractual agreement drawn up by the AO that an EQA would have to sign prior to commencing in the role.

Irrespective of sector, EQAs must have a range of qualities, skills and abilities in order to be effective in the role. These are outlined below.

Think about how you can demonstrate your qualities, skills and abilities to your AO if you are applying to become an EQA.

1   **Integrity** – which by its very nature causes some headaches for inexperienced EQAs. When they start in the role they need a well-developed understanding of integrity and its importance, but also an awareness of how it can create pitfalls and compromise them in their work. These are some of the major areas of concern:

- EQAs have to be able to be firm but pleasant and stand by their decisions. They must be sufficiently strong in character not to let their opinions about the centre staff or their dislike of conflict deflect them from their decisions. However, every EQA will find that they also need to be flexible and reasonable in the role, and these (sometimes conflicting) requirements can be difficult to balance. When determining whether to stand by a decision or to be flexible, EQAs will always, as a final consideration, explore whether the learners have been disadvantaged by what the centre has done (or not done) and whether at any point the integrity of the qualification has been compromised. If the answer to both these questions is 'no', then there is room for the EQA to be flexible. However, if the answer to one or both is 'yes', there is no room for the EQA to give ground.

- All EQAs have to be able to identify conflicts of interest – for example, if they already work as a team member at a centre in a particular locality, then carrying out the quality assurance of other centres delivering the same programmes/qualifications in the area may not be a good idea – particularly if the centres could be perceived as 'competitors' in any way. This is because if, as a result of a sample, the EQA had to make an unpopular decision, the centre being sampled might then suspect the motives of the EQA whose own centre they perceive to be in competition with them. It is the EQA's responsibility to immediately inform the AO of any conflicts of interest – preferably before they start working with a centre – and any that may subsequently arise.

- EQAs cannot sell services or products to centres and continue to be the EQA for that centre. So, for example, if a centre requested that an EQA carry out some training for them the EQA must agree this with the AO. The AO will then manage this process by agreeing a price with the centre and a fee with the EQA. However, if the EQA decides that they want to carry out this work privately and directly with the centre, then they must inform the AO and the AO will allocate a different EQA to work with the centre.
- EQAs cannot accept favours, services, goods or money from centres. If an EQA is offered anything like this then they must inform the AO before agreeing to accept them. The AO is likely to instruct the EQA not to accept.
- EQAs must not use their own standards or the standards in their own centre as the benchmark for other centres. If a centre is meeting the requirements of a programme/qualification, then that is sufficient. Many EQAs initially find this a difficult area. It is acceptable – desirable – to explain or show centres how to improve their practice, even if they are already meeting the requirements. However, it is not acceptable to penalise a centre for not meeting one's own personal standards. The EQA role is to support centres to meet the requirements as specified by the AO for any given programme/qualification and, where possible, improve the practice of centre staff. There is no place for EQAs to use personal standards and to impose additional or alternative requirements on centres.
- Details relating to a particular centre, its staff, programmes, qualifications, resources – all information – must be held confidentially by the EQA. The only people appropriate to share information with are AO staff. This can be more difficult than it sounds, particularly when the EQA is trying to explain to another centre how to implement improvements but also trying not to divulge where the good ideas originated!

2 **Being well organised** is a huge bonus to an EQA, as the role requires good practice in:
- the storage and use of information
- managing time
- self-management in general
- prioritising importance
- locating premises.

All of which are baseline requirements in the role.

3 **Planning** is a fundamental part of what the EQA has to be able to do – this is covered in depth from page 118.

4   **Analytical skills, managing information and being able to prioritise** are very important, as the EQA has to process a lot of information before, during and after the sampling activity. The information analysed by the EQA will include numerical data, dates, technical information and audit trails, from plans through to records provided by the centre and examples of the learner's work. The information is likely to be a mixture of electronic, paper and verbal data. Some of it will originate in the centre, some will come from the AO and some will be held by the EQA themselves.

Before sampling of activities – both in the form of a visit or a remote sample – can take place, the EQA has to analyse information from the AO and the centre. They then have to prioritise it in order to be able to produce a plan for the sample (see page 118).

During the visit or remote sample, the EQA will be absorbing and analysing a lot of data in quick succession as the centre attempts to show them everything that they can to demonstrate that they are meeting the requirements. During a visit is probably the most challenging time to analyse data, as often the centre staff are talking while the EQA is reading written or electronic information.

EQAs quickly learn to identify where a problem lies. They then need to be able to prioritise what they will do to investigate the issue, what are the most urgent actions required of the centre and the level of importance of each.

In addition, the EQA will be required to complete some form of documentation recording what they have sampled, their opinion of it, what met the requirements and what did not. To do this in an accurate and time-efficient way, they will need to be able to quickly analyse information, distill it down to the most salient points and again prioritise these for inclusion in the report.

Prioritising actions for the centre can be crucial. If a centre has a lot of areas that require development they may have a very long action plan in which the most crucial actions can seem of the same importance as others. In this situation the EQA may make a decision to record some of the less important actions in the report, but action plan for the most crucial ones only. They would need to discuss this with the centre to explain what they have done and the possible impact that this may have.

EQAs should complete the report while on the visit in order to be able to read back to the centre the 'sense' of what the report contains at the closing meeting. However, following the visit, most EQAs usually proofread and finalise their report, and they may have to analyse any additional information provided by the centre which they did not have time to consider or was not available during the time of the sample. They would then have to decide if this information needs to be included or if it results in a change to the actions in the report.

5 **Assertiveness, good communication skills and the ability to negotiate** – these include being able to manage the relationship with the centre, lead the sampling visit itself and clearly lead what happens during the day. For the EQA, being assertive requires a positive attitude, an ability to be firm, stay calm and to remain professional – sometimes when under pressure.

Managing the relationship with the centre requires good communication skills from the start to ensure clarity and professionalism. All communication with centres is – from their standpoint – communication from the AO and not from the EQA personally. So there is a real need for the EQA to be sure that what they are saying is accurate, up to date and contains only what the AO would be able to confirm. This needs to be in the forefront of an EQA's mind at all times.

It is also useful for EQAs to remember that anything they write to a team member at a centre will often be treated as being 'written in tablets of stone' and can be used as if it were a directive from the AO. All emails sent by EQAs should be prepared with this in mind.

Also, many emails sent by an EQA to a centre are forwarded on – as they stand – to senior managers and others inside and outside the centre, and will often be used to justify actions that the centre subsequently takes. Therefore, again, all written communication should be produced with this possibility in mind. Emails in particular – but all written communication with others – should be composed in relatively formal language, and contain only information that is accurate, up to date and representative of what the AO (not the EQA personally) is trying to convey.

From the start of the relationship, the EQA needs to establish that they will be professional, practical and positive, and all their communication should demonstrate this. So making the first contact and organising the first activity should be done with this in mind.

Communication between EQAs and centres takes place between samples when queries arise at the centre or information is forwarded by the EQA. Again, this needs to be done in a professional and positive way.

On an ongoing basis, often centres will need to rearrange or postpone arrangements made during the previous sample. So, although a date may have tentatively been set for the next action, as the date approaches it may not be the most sensible way forward. For example, if the centre has had no new learners since the last EQA action it might be a waste of time to go ahead with the planned sample. In this situation the EQA – in agreement with the AO – would probably postpone and rearrange the visit. They may need to be assertive in making these arrangements – for example, to ensure that the centre does not delay the sample too long. This process of negotiation must always be led by the EQA on behalf of the AO.

However, no EQA should feel pressurised by a centre, as the EQA is only *recommending* the actions that should be taken by the AO or the centre. The role of an EQA is to recommend action based on what they have found. It is the AO who takes the decision about what they or the centre should do – or stop doing. If an EQA feels uncertain about what they should do or are feeling that they are in a difficult position with the centre, they should contact the AO and explain the situation. In such cases it is usually a joint decision as to what action the EQA should take next. This can on occasion result in the EQA withdrawing from the centre and abandoning the visit.

It is important that the EQA commences their relationship with a centre from a positive starting point. The details of the centre will be sent to the EQA and the centre will be informed that the EQA will be in touch with them – often within 10 days. It is therefore crucial that the EQA does make contact within the specified timescale.

*'Diplomacy, n. is
the art of letting
somebody else have
your way.'*
David Frost

6 **Diplomacy** is one of the most difficult skills to define when teasing out the qualities, skills and abilities that an EQA needs, as it is most easy to identify when it is not being used! To summarise – diplomacy is the art of getting the message across tactfully and without giving offence. It is directly related to being assertive.

In all communication, EQAs need to be diplomatic and non-personal while also being assertive and clear in what they say to centres. The power of the communication will be lost if the recipient is personally offended by how it is phrased and does not know what to do to recover their position. In this situation they will often get angry.

It is therefore important that all communication from an EQA is phrased in ways that will clearly get the message across while not causing personal offence. Also it is very useful, wherever possible, if the EQA can suggest possible courses of action that will enable the centre to improve their practice and meet the requirements.

ACTIVITY

Think about the following statements. Rewrite them to make them more diplomatic and positive while still getting the message across.

1   Your assessment records are rubbish. They don't contain nearly enough detail. Even the 'who, what, where and when' are missing.
2   I don't think this person should be on the team. They haven't been an IQA for years and their CPD is out of date.
3   Your team has not got a clue what is required on this qualification.

See page 219 for suggested responses.

So, as can be seen in the suggested answers, even the most unpalatable information can be transmitted in a way that limits the offence it will cause and, most importantly, also provides a number of positive ways forward for the recipient.

This approach means that the centre knows what is expected of the team involved, they have been offered support and they have not been personally affronted by what has been said.

It enables the EQA to move forward positively with the centre while being sure that they have made clear:

- which areas need to be developed
- where good practice has taken place
- what can be done by the centre to make progress
- what the EQA and the AO can do to help
- that timescales need to be set
- that (if appropriate) Direct Claims Status (DCS) cannot be recommended at this time (DCS is where a centre can claim certificates without the work having to be sampled by an EQA beforehand; the EQA may, however, select it at the next sample).

7   **Feedback skills** – are a fundamental part of what the EQA has to be able to do and are covered in depth from page 153.

8   **Accurate recording** – is also a major skill that EQAs need and it is covered in depth on page 164.

As can be seen above, to be a successful EQA requires that the person enters the role with a highly developed set of qualities, skills and abilities that can be further honed and augmented while in the role.

These qualities, in addition to the need for the EQA to have a wealth of technical experience to draw upon alongside confidence in themselves and their work, explain why most EQAs tend to have reached senior positions in their organisations.

BECOMING AN EQA – RECRUITMENT AND INDUCTION

EQAs are generally recruited and selected by an AO to carry out the role outlined on pages 99 and 111.

In most cases, interested people – who are usually experienced tutors/assessors/IQAs in their own organisation or in their sector – apply by forwarding their CV and qualifications to an AO and expressing an interest in becoming an EQA. If or when a vacancy occurs, the applicant is then contacted, interviewed and, if successful, inducted into the AO's working practices.

Sometimes an experienced and talented person may be spotted by an AO representative and encouraged to apply to join the EQA team.

In the vast majority of cases EQAs are part-time contracted members of the AO team. In the main they are not usually members of an AO's core staff.

One of the reasons for this is that EQAs are required to keep their knowledge and competence up to date. One of the best ways of ensuring that this happens is by EQAs remaining involved in the delivery of the qualifications that they then go on to monitor. If they are part-time contracted workers then they are able to continue as practitioners as well as being EQAs.

Another reason for this arrangement is that EQAs may only carry out sampling activities once each year on each programme or qualification in each centre. So in many cases there would not be sufficient work for a full-time post.

However, some AOs take the view that having a small team of EQAs who are full-time members of staff enables them to invest more in them to ensure that their practice is at the topmost level. They also feel that this gives them greater control over how centres are monitored. Different AOs inevitably have different approaches.

When taken on as a contractor, the new EQA is assumed to be 'up to speed' in terms of their technical, assessment and internal quality assurance practice. So the AO focuses on developing their EQA skills. The new EQA usually starts by learning the processes of their particular AO and may have a series of support activities directed by their manager or co-ordinator.

ACTIVITY

What sorts of activities do you think a new EQA might undertake to become familiar with the role?

In most cases, AOs will arrange a variety of activities for their fledgling EQAs – very similar to those undertaken by any new recruit starting in any organisation. So this may include being:

- initially assessed
- taken through an induction session
- given material to read about the AO and the EQA role
- 'buddied' with an experienced EQA
- introduced to the required paperwork
- familiarised with the policies and procedures
- introduced to other team members
- briefed about how legislation such as Health and Safety, Equality and Data Protection might affect the role
- taken on a visit to observe an experienced EQA

- accompanied on their first visit by an experienced person
- required to attend training, eg good practice in recording
- started on a relevant (ie EQA) qualification.

This induction process may take a few months to complete. There are a number of reasons for this, including practical realities, such as:
- most AOs do not recruit large numbers of EQAs, so induction sessions are not likely to be held every month; it is common for a new recruit to have to wait a few months until the next induction is due
- there may be a time lapse before a suitably experienced EQA has a visit planned that the new recruit can observe
- the new recruit may have commitments in their other work that they need to fulfil before they can commence
- they may not be allocated to centres immediately on being recruited so cannot be accompanied until this is done.

So during the initial few months following recruitment, the new EQA's time is spent – as with most new recruits to any organisation – learning the basic requirements, being 'shepherded' by more experienced people and acclimatising to the new role.

The amount of time that lapses between the point at which the new EQA is recruited and when they take their first actions as an EQA differs according to a range of factors. For example, if the new recruit is taking over from an experienced EQA who has retired or resigned in a planned way, then they may have recently completed a round of visits and the new EQA will find that they are not required to take any further action for six to twelve months.

This will also depend upon the requirements of the programme/qualification being quality assured. In some sectors, EQA sampling is only required once a year, so again there could feasibly be a period of up to 12 months where the EQA is allocated to a centre but is not required to carry out any activity.

Many centres develop to a point where they are allowed to claim certificates without an EQA sampling the work. This is often known as Direct Claims Status (DCS). This usually means that the centre has:
- a good track record in delivering the programme/qualification
- previous EQAs have not identified any significant issues in relation to the way that the programme/qualification is being delivered
- there were no sanctions raised against the centre in relation to this programme/qualification at the last EQA visit
- the team has consistently shown integrity in how it delivers the programme/qualification.

As a result of achieving one or more of the above, the centre would then be allowed to claim certificates without an EQA sampling the work.

Please note that DCS is not allowed on most new programmes or qualifications until there has been a satisfactory sample of that programme/qualification carried out by an EQA.

So the newly recruited EQA may find that there is a period of up to a year until they need to make a visit to a particular centre.

However, on occasion, the new recruit will find that the centres are awaiting a visit and are anxious for arrangements to be made. For example, the centre may need a visit at fairly short notice because:

- They have been inactive for a while but have now registered learners.
- Their previous EQA left suddenly and it has taken some time for the AO to identify a suitable replacement EQA.
- There have been changes to the requirements contained in the programme/qualifications and so DCS is not allowed. The centre will therefore not be able to claim certificates without a sample being carried out by an EQA and all requirements found to be met. This is particularly pertinent if the centre claims funding based on the achievement of the qualification. The centre will often then pressurise the AO to send in an EQA quickly.
- The AO previously had no one able to carry out the sample due to other conditions. For example, if the centre has requested that the EQA be a fluent Welsh speaker or if they are geographically remote (such as a centre in the Scottish Highlands or Islands), then the AO may have had difficulties in finding a suitable EQA. This can result in the new recruit – if they can meet the additional conditions – being allocated to the centre and carrying out sampling earlier than would otherwise be the case.

So some newly recruited FQAs may find themselves active before the completion of the induction process. However, they will be supported through this period by their line manager or the co-ordinator who is responsible for them. In addition, AO staff would understand if the new EQA was to say that they do not feel ready, confident or sufficiently competent to start working with a centre and taking appropriate action.

RESPONSIBILITIES OF AN EQA

[6312 unit 404 AC1.1]

The EQA has responsibility for a range of actions before, during and after a visit or a remote sample. These responsibilities differ according to the type of sampling activity undertaken.

In the time that an EQA spends working with a centre, they may be required to advise managers, support staff members, be a conduit for information or listen to an appeal.

Agree all actions with your AO representative before carrying them out.

However, in general terms the main responsibilities of an EQA are:

- **Maintaining communication with centres.** This starts with the first contact, where the EQA introduces themselves, through to the final contact when the centre is allocated to another EQA or ceases to be active. On an ongoing basis most communication is carried out during a visit, but it also continues between samples, and is then usually via email or phone. Good, positive communication – both written and verbal – is very important in all communication with centres.
- **Evaluating and approving centres to deliver qualifications** – this involves all the activities outlined on page 116.
- **Ensuring centre staff interpret, understand and apply the requirements** specified in the programmes or qualifications that their learners are working towards. This commences at approval and is the main focus of the ongoing monitoring that EQAs carry out.
- **Planning and carrying out sampling of assessed work.** Exactly as with IQA work, the EQA has to plan and carry out the sampling process in a systematic and methodical way that ensures a representative sample takes place.
- **Monitoring internal quality assurance practice.** The EQA mainly focuses their monitoring on the sampling that has been planned and carried out by the IQA. This is because the IQA has the opportunity to sample the work of tutors and assessors on a regular basis. The EQA has only limited opportunities for sampling and so in the main follows the audit trail laid by the IQA.
- **Monitoring the way learning is facilitated.** The EQA will examine course outlines, schemes of work, sessions plans, etc, to ensure that requirements are being met and the learners are progressing as expected.
- **Monitoring learning delivery.** In addition to sampling the IQA's work in monitoring quality, the EQA will look directly at how the learning is delivered. This may involve an EQA carrying out an observation of a learning session being delivered.

- **Evaluating the knowledge, skills and competence of potential centre staff members.** Whenever new people are needed to join a centre team, the IQA is responsible for determining whether applicants meet the requirements, as this is a centre management issue. However, the EQA does have a role in confirming the decision taken by the IQA, and can refuse to accept someone onto the list of approved tutors or assessors if they are unable to meet – or prove that they meet – the requirements.

- **Interviewing learners and others – including team members.** This enables the EQA to confirm information that has been given to them by the centre managers and team members.

- **Monitoring assessment practice.** This is done using a range of techniques that might include observing an assessment taking place and interviewing learners.

- **Providing advice, guidance, information and support to centres.** An EQA is often a major source of information to a centre. The EQA can send information to the centre, forward it from other sources, point out sources such as websites and keep centres informed about developments in the sector.

- **Documenting the external quality assurance process and decisions.** EQAs carry out samples and monitor practice in their work with centres. However, it is crucial that their reporting skills are good and that they keep detailed notes, otherwise the centre will not have an accurate record of what was found and subsequently agreed – and neither will the AO (see page 164).

- **Identifying issues and trends.** EQAs are in a unique position to note common issues and trends in how qualifications are delivered in centres. This is because they are very often the only people who regularly monitor the same and related qualifications in different centres and different locations.

- **Providing feedback to IQAs.** EQAs can give an objective insight into IQA practice – and this is often invaluable for IQAs who work alone and have no colleague IQAs in their sector or centre. They can also share good practice and alert IQAs to pitfalls that they have seen in other centres – while of course maintaining confidentiality.

- **Advising and supporting IQAs and assessors.** EQAs provide the most direct support and advice to team members in centres. They can provide technical guidance and advice about working methods that centres are not able to get anywhere else.

- **Monitoring standardisation activities to ensure accuracy and consistency of assessment decisions within and between centres.** EQAs – as stated before – are often the only people who monitor in detail the same programmes or qualifications across a range of centres. They can assist centres to standardise among their own staff, and can guide centres to standardise approaches using methods that they have seen elsewhere.

- **Reviewing centre developments and progress.** The EQA has an opportunity to support centres by reviewing their developments and giving them feedback. In many cases EQAs can also suggest further adjustments to support the improvement of quality in the centre.
- **Taking part in CPD.** EQAs have to complete CPD on a number of levels. They need to keep their technical knowledge of their subject up to date, and they have to keep up to date with EQA practice, but they must also be up to date with developments in assessment and IQA practice (see page180).
- **Maintaining communication with AO staff.** EQAs are managed by members of the AO staff team. They will often have a primary person to whom they report and others who might be subject specialists or who are responsible for particular centres that the EQA monitors.

EQAs are also sometimes required to:
- **Deal with assessment appeals and complaints**. Most EQAs are never called upon to hear or take part in appeals against assessment decisions or complaints. This is because most complaints do not become formal issues and are dealt with by centres using the most informal processes possible. However, very occasionally an EQA may be asked to give a view on a situation or to review a complaint. They would not do this in isolation – they would be guided by their manager or co-ordinator and by the policies and processes of the AO.
- **Liaise with others involved in the external quality assurance process, eg systems consultants.** In some AOs, an EQA might carry out the entire role of quality assurance monitoring. This includes sampling systems that are not directly involved in the delivery of the programme or qualification but that support the wider organisation – for example, how the centre manages CPD, the candidate tracking systems it uses or the content of its policies and procedures. In other AOs the role is split into EQAs who carry out technical monitoring of how programmes or qualifications are delivered and Systems Consultants who audit everything else. Liaising with other people who are also monitoring the centre is something many EQAs have to manage.
- **Carry out visits at short notice to assist in an investigation**. A small number of EQAs may be asked to carry out a short notice visit or even to visit on an unannounced basis. This visit may be carried out as a result of concerns raised by another EQA and is therefore an informal exploration of what has happened, or it may be because a formal investigation is taking place into how a centre is operating.

Some of these responsibilities are explored further in the coming sections of this book.

ACTIVITY

You have now read about the responsibilities of an EQA. Before you progress to the next section think about visits made to your centre by your EQA. Try to recall the kinds of activities you have seen them use to monitor:

- quality of learning
- reliability of assessment decisions
- fairness in learning.

Try to identify two activities that they might do in relation to each.

In your answer you might have identified some of the following:

- Quality of learning:
  observation of learning delivery
  examination of course materials
  discussions with tutors
  discussions with learners
  examination of learner work.

- Reliability of assessment decisions:
  examination of assessment plans
  examination of assessment records
  observation of an assessment – including feedback
  examination of learner work
  discussions with assessors
  discussions with IQAs.

- Fairness in learning
  examination of IQA monitoring – retention, completion and achievement rates, etc
  examination of IQA processes, plans and samples
  discussions with IQAs, tutors and assessors
  discussions with learners
  examination of all plans and records.

These EQA techniques are considered in more detail in the following sections of this book.

THE QUALITY ASSURANCE STARTING POINT

Quality assurance starts for most EQAs when they first receive notification that they have been allocated to a centre. In some cases an EQA may 'inherit' an existing centre and will be picking up on work already completed by the previous EQA. They would receive copies of reports and may have an opportunity to discuss the centre with the previous EQA and AO staff.

However, for many EQAs the relationship with a centre commences when they are asked to carry out an approval process with an organisation that has applied to offer qualifications accredited by an AO. This approval activity can be done by conducting a visit to a centre, or it can be completed remotely by reviewing application documents that the centre has submitted. This is often known as a desk-based approval.

Initially the organisation may need to apply to become a centre in its own right, and so will complete an application specifically designed to test its readiness to become a centre.

ACTIVITY

Think about a centre that needs to prove it is capable of delivering qualifications. What do you think are the main factors that an EQA looks for?

1

2

3

4

You may have identified some or all of the points below. Irrespective of whether the organisation is applying to become a centre in the first instance or if it is already a centre and is now applying to deliver a specific qualification, during the approval process the EQA investigates whether it can meet the sorts of requirements shown in the following table:

Requirement	What this might include
Management principles and systems	• policies such as those related to Equality and Diversity, Health and Safety, or Safeguarding • procedures for managing disputes, appeals, grievances, special assessment requirements • appeals log • plans for communication inside the centre • schedules of planned meetings.
Resources	• people – viewing CVs, original certificates • viewing facilities • viewing equipment • discussing materials.
Support for learners	Description or example of: • induction • learner handbook • programme outline • action plan and review documents.
Assessment	Description or example of: • documentation • assessment methods • assessment tools • assessment criteria.
Internal quality assurance	Description or examples of: • quality Systems • planning processes • mechanisms for supporting team members • standardisation activities.
Continuous improvement systems	Description or examples of: • reviews of team members development needs • programme reviews • quality improvement plans • CPD planning and records • policy reviews • evaluation processes.
Suitable record-keeping processes	Description or example of: • learner information • IQA records • team member records • secure storage • minutes of meetings.

Often the section on 'Resources' is the most important – and, of these, the available human resources are of primary importance. In many cases centres may be able to gain approval to deliver programmes and qualifications even though they have an action plan outlining some areas where they need to develop further. But in order to gain approval they must have identified appropriate staff resources and be able to present details of them at the point of approval.

In addition, to ensure that this crucial requirement for human resources is met, most EQAs prefer to interview or at least meet prospective team members as well as examine their CVs and original certificates. It is the responsibility of the IQA to put forward appropriate people to join the team and the EQA then reviews the information provided to check that the proposed people can meet the specific requirements of the programme or qualification.

If staff resources meet the requirements, then different EQAs may scrutinise and pay most attention to different areas in an approval process dependent upon the programme or qualification that the centre is hoping to deliver. For example, when visiting a centre that had applied to deliver an engineering programme or qualification, the EQA would probably be focused on the required equipment being available to learners, and Health and Safety arrangements. However, if the centre had applied to deliver qualifications in customer service – although the EQA would still to an extent consider equipment and Health and Safety – the main focus of the visit might be more on learner support, for example.

In all cases the EQA would ask to see what the centre already has in place or request that the centre staff explain their plans to work towards meeting the requirements. In any areas where development was still needed – but it was not sufficiently significant to hold up approval – an action plan would be agreed.

So a centre might gain approval and yet have an action plan to develop in certain areas. They would also agree dates(s) for completing the actions. Progress on achieving the action plan would then be the first part of the monitoring undertaken at the first visit after approval.

At the end of the visit, if approval is not recommended then the organisation and the EQA will agree an action plan with a review date. The agreed date may be weeks or months from the original approval visit, depending on the amount of work required to complete the action plan.

Most reviews tend to be planned for three to six months after the initial visit to allow the centre sufficient time in which to fully comply with the requirements. The further review may be another visit, or could also be completed by doing a 'remote' or desk-based sample.

PLANNING AND PREPARATION FOR EQA ACTIVITIES [6312 unit 404 AC2.1]

Give yourself plenty of time to plan before the required deadline. The EQA planning process often takes longer than you would expect.

In the previous section you have read a description of what happens when an EQA carries out an approval of a centre. When an EQA is taking over an existing centre, the process is somewhat different.

The EQA is usually approached by their contact at the AO and a request is made for them to commence monitoring a particular centre. The EQA may be given a set of documents produced by the centre's previous EQA, but if this is not possible then the EQA may be given contact details only. The AO contact would also indicate when the next EQA activity is required for the centre. Often the AO contact will ask the EQA to make contact in the next few weeks and aim to carry out a visit within a specified timescale.

It is at this point that the EQA will phone or email the centre, introduce themselves to the named person – who is likely to be an IQA or QAC/IQAC – and request to make a visit. At this point the EQA is likely to suggest and agree a date and provide information about what the sample will contain and who will need to be present during the day.

Following this less formal contact, most AOs have forms to complete in order to:
- confirm the appointed date of the visit
- request learner data from which the EQA will select the sample
- plan out the visit itself.

Alternatively, if the EQA has visited the centre before, they will already have agreed the next visit date. The EQA will have diarised the proposed date and then, approximately 8 weeks in advance, they will complete and send documents similar to those described below.

THE INITIAL PLANNING DOCUMENT [6312 unit 404 AC2.2]

The initial document that the EQA usually sends to the centre confirms the date of the visit and requests information from the centre. It will usually have sections that record some or all of the following:

Name and address of centre, contact details, centre number

EQA name, address, phone number, email address, etc

Confirmation of agreed date and start time

Request for information about:
- learners
- internal quality assurance plans
- internal quality assurance sampling
- tutors and assessors

A target date for returning the information to the EQA

Any additional comments

When the centre receives the confirmation they will then put together the requested information and return it to the EQA.

The EQA will await the return of the information. If it does not appear by the agreed date, the EQA is likely to contact the centre again to check that they received the confirmation document and to remind the centre about the need to provide the data.

When they receive the information, the EQA may check the AO's recording system to ensure that the information stored there matches what the centre has provided. If there are anomalies, the EQA may contact the centre or their AO contact to identify and confirm which set of data is the most accurate. When they are satisfied that they have the entire picture they will then plan the visit and the sample based on what they now know to be current data.

EQA VISIT PLANNING [6312 unit 404 AC2.2 & AC2.3]

The EQA will use the information that the AO can provide along with that provided by the centre to plan out the practicalities of the visit. They will send this plan off to the centre at the earliest opportunity. This enables and encourages the centre to fully prepare for the visit and what is required.

Most AOs have a document or form for planning out a visit. These will usually have sections that record some or all of the following:

Name and address of centre, contact details, centre number
EQA name, address, phone number, email address, etc
Confirmation of agreed date and start time
Qualifications to be sampled at the visit
An outline plan for the day
Team members who need to be available to meet the EQA on the day
Details of the learners and qualifications that will be sampled – including those who will be interviewed or observed
Details of assessors and IQAs allocated to the learners
Details of assessment sites
Request for the EQA to carry out an observation of IQA and/or assessment practice
Any additional comments

When the EQA has planned the outline of the visit they then concentrate on planning the actual sample.

ACTIVITY [6312 unit 404 AC3.2]

Think about an external quality assurance visit that you have had to your centre. What are the main areas checked during the process?

The main areas that the external quality assurance process is designed to check are:
- required internal systems are in place – such as management and administration
- suitable resources are available – people, equipment, machinery, premises, etc
- learning and training are of a high standard, meet all requirements and are monitored internally
- learning delivery, assessment and IQA practice are in line with the current NOS for these activities
- learning delivery, assessment and IQA practice are in line with the relevant assessment strategy
- learning and assessment are planned and systematically carried out
- learners are inducted and supported throughout and their individual needs considered
- assessment takes place as required in the programme/ qualification specification

- internal quality assurance systems are fit for purpose and do actually monitor the quality of the 'learner journey'
- internal quality assurance sampling is planned for and carried out throughout the 'learner journey' and not just at the end of the process
- tutors and assessors are supported, given feedback on their practice and take part in standardisation activities
- tutors and assessors are regularly observed carrying out training and assessment processes
- all members of the team maintain their CPD and keep CPD records
- record keeping is maintained as required
- communication with others – such as the AO – is effective
- centres review their activities and take action to improve their programmes and practice.

The areas that the process is designed to check and the techniques that EQAs use are discussed further on page 139.

EXTERNAL QUALITY ASSURANCE SAMPLE PLANNING [6312 unit 404 AC.3.1]

If you have not read Part 2 of this book (which covers internal quality assurance) you might find it useful just to read through pages 37 to 41 about sampling prior to continuing with this chapter.

Most AOs have some form of document that EQAs are required to use to plan their sample. This is where they would give the centre the details of what and who has to be available on the day of the visit/remote sample. The form will usually include information about what type of sampling is going to be carried out and what activities the EQA needs to observe (see page 139 for possible EQA sampling techniques).

The EQA will plan their sample on a very similar basis to a sample planned by an IQA. So if they were a City & Guilds EQA, they would use an agreed rationale as a base for planning the sample of a tutor/assessor's work. They would use a slightly adapted version of CAMERA (see page 41), which requires that EQAs select a representative sample that includes something from all different types of:
- **C**andidates/learners
- **A**ssessors/tutors/IQAs
- **M**ethods of learning delivery/assessment
- **E**vidence
- **R**ecords
- **A**ssessment sites

From their external standpoint, the EQA will ensure over a period of time (for example, over two years or three visits) that they sample something from all the assessors in the centre, from all the IQAs, all the sites, etc. Their sample will also aim to follow the sampling carried out by the IQAs in the centre. So the EQA will use the IQA sample plans and records, and will plan for their sample to monitor what the IQA had originally planned and then carried out, and that the records that they have received are accurate.

As with internal quality assurance the plan will include different types of sampling, such as those outlined in the activity below.

ACTIVITY [6312 unit 404 AC3.1]

If you have already done this exercise in the IQA section of this book then use this as a refresher activity.

If you have not completed the IQA version of this activity then here are the main types of EQA sampling. What do you think the following terms mean? Try to complete the definitions:

Interim sampling takes
place..

Vertical sampling is where the EQA
samples..

Horizontal sampling is where the EQA
samples..

Theme-based sampling is where the EQA
samples..

Summative sampling takes
place..

Now look at the following definitions..

See page 221 for answers.

So the EQA will be planning to carry out one or more of the types of sampling outlined above as they plan to sample:

- some incomplete programmes and/or qualifications, ie interim sampling
- some complete programmes or qualifications, ie summative sampling
- all parts of the programme or qualification over a period of time, eg over two years or over three visits
- some work that has been undertaken by all team members
- a variety of types of learner work
- a range of records.

In addition, the EQA will be planning the techniques that they will use to carry out the sample (see page 139 for EQA sampling techniques). So the plan will tell the centre which documents and learner materials they will need to make available. It will also tell them if they need to have additional learner work available for the EQA to extend the sample during the day to include learners who have not been specified on the planning documents.

The plan will also include the names of people whom the EQA intends to interview, an outline of the IQA and assessment practice that they intend to observe, and possibly additional people whom they may request to meet during the visit – such as senior managers or assessors from other sites.

When considering what to include in the sample the EQA will also be taking other issues into account, and will largely take decisions about what to focus on based on a risk assessment of the centre.

RISK MANAGEMENT [6312 unit 404 AC3.1]

In order to effectively target support and resources when planning and undertaking any form of monitoring, EQAs base their visit plans and samples on an assessment of the risk inherent in the centre.

The EQA might have gathered information about the risk in the centre from previous experience of monitoring there, from AO staff, from a previous EQA, from approving the centre initially or by asking questions of the centre staff. They will then use this information to inform the type and amount of sampling undertaken and the techniques used. The risk assessment might also have an impact on which sampling techniques are used, where it is carried out, who is included, etc.

The kind of information that an EQA would consider as part of a risk assessment might include:
- level of complexity of the centre model
- level of experience and maturity of organisation
- centre track record in general
- previous tariffs the centre has had
- experience, workload and location of IQAs, assessors and tutors
- stability of the centre or qualification team
- any known 'problem' units
- number of qualification routes or subjects being delivered
- types of assessment methods used and evidence available
- number of assessment sites
- number of learners
- types of records kept.

ACTIVITY [6312 unit 404 AC3.1]

Think about your own centre or one that you know. Consider the risk areas that are itemised on page 123. Where are the highest areas of risk in the centre?

Prioritise the risk against the factors below as you would if you were the EQA planning a sample there.

You can grade the risk in the box as **H – High, M – Medium** or **L – Low**

H/M/L

1   Experience, workload and location of IQAs and assessors involved

2   Stability of the centre or qualification team

3   Any known 'problem' units

4   Levels of complexity in the centre model

5   Number of qualification routes or subjects being delivered

6   Types of assessment methods used and evidence available

7   Number of assessment sites

8   Number of learners

9   Types of records kept

10 Level of experience and maturity of organisation

Now think about planning a sample – if you were the EQA, what might you include in your plan or do differently as a result of your risk analysis?

So an EQA will base their sample on a sound rationale, assess the risk and determine where to focus their activities in the same way as an IQA would. They will then inform the centre of what they will be sampling using the AO document, the typical content of which is outlined on page 120.

An EQA's overall sample plan document for a centre will sometimes look like one that an IQA would use. But this one is maintained by the EQA, and is not a document that is usually required by the AO.

PLANNING AND PREPARATION FOR A REMOTE SAMPLE [6312 unit 404 AC2.2 & AC2.3]

Remote (sometimes known as desk-based) sampling takes place and can be very useful in a number of situations – for example, where a centre:

- is well established and has a good track record
- had no action points at the last visit

- has had no change of staff since the last visit
- has low numbers of learners
- carries out regular reviews and introduces year-on-year improvements
- is geographically remote and has low numbers of learners
- does not have DCS and requests an early sample of a small number of learners
- requests an early EQA sample to gain feedback on their delivery of a new programme.

So if one or more of the above applies to a centre, the EQA may plan and carry out a remote sample in place of a visit. They will sample documents, materials and learner work in their own premises or at the AO's offices and they will not travel to the centre being sampled.

For the EQA, in many ways planning a remote sample is very similar to planning a visit. They will use the same sound rationale and make decisions based on an assessment of the risk in the programme/ qualification at the centre.

The EQA will contact the centre, agree the date of the sample, confirm this and await the information that they need to plan the sample. They will then plan what the sample will contain in the same way that they would for a visit (see page 120) and send the plan to the Centre Contact. The planning document will be similar to that for a visit, though instead of listing people to be met it will outline whom the EQA needs to contact by phone and it will not include a plan for the day itself. So typically the planning document for a remote sample would contain the following information:

Name and address of centre, contact details, centre number
EQA name, phone number, email address and postal address where the centre will send the requested documents and materials
Confirmation of agreed date for the sample
Qualifications to be sampled
Team members who might need to be available to speak by phone to the EQA on the day
Details of the learners and qualifications that will be sampled – including those who might be interviewed by phone
Details of assessors and IQAs allocated to the learners
Details of assessment sites
Any additional comments – such as delivery instructions for the documents and materials

Most EQAs will request receipt of the documents and materials a few days prior to when they plan to carry out the sample in order to allow for any delays in delivery. The EQA will then await delivery of the documents and materials in readiness for the day when they will carry out the sample.

On the agreed date the EQA will sample from the documents and materials provided, and if they have any queries or want to discuss the materials further they will phone or email the Centre Contact/relevant IQA to progress. The EQA will monitor some of the same areas and will usually complete similar documentation as if they were carrying out a visit to a centre. They may also give a verbal summary of what they have found to the Centre Contact/IQA by phone prior to submitting their report to the AO.

Some points about remote sampling

As we have seen above, remote sampling can be a very useful tool for both centres and the AO. However, most EQAs (and centres) prefer centre visits to remote sampling.

Often, if the EQA finds issues or omissions in records or learner work during a remote sample, they will not be as confident in reporting this back to the centre or AO. This is because there is a risk that the EQA may have misunderstood or misconstrued what they have been sent and therefore their judgement – made on an isolated basis – may not be fair or representative of how the centre works. This often means that during a remote sample EQAs spend time on the phone to the centre trying to clarify what has been sent and ensuring that they have not misunderstood anything.

When arranging a remote sample of an e-portfolio, request access before the date of the planned sample so that you have time to familiarise yourself with the format.

So sometimes EQAs and centres do not find remote sampling as useful as an EQA visit and will request that a planned remote sample be converted into a routine EQA visit at the premises. The main concerns that EQAs and centres raise in relation to remote sampling are:

- the risk of learner work getting lost in the mail
- the EQA cannot give the centre as detailed an update on developments in the AO and in relation to the programmes/qualifications being sampled
- there is not enough opportunity for either party to ask questions
- issues with delivery, such as parcels being held up at a courier depot that is miles from its destination, parcels arriving after the agreed date of the sample or not arriving at all

- the EQA may be more likely to give action points, as some issues that could be resolved at a visit remain issues when being remotely sampled – for example, if the EQA cannot navigate through the learner's work when sampling at a centre (though not an ideal situation) a member of staff would assist; during a remote sample the EQA may simply not be able to find what they are looking for and give an action point to the centre instructing them to improve referencing and clarify audit trails (it is the responsibility of the centre to ensure that EQAs can easily follow referencing systems and audit trails)
- the centre misses out on the opportunity to learn from and 'pick the brains' of their EQA.

Major improvements in technology (such as e-portfolios) are already overcoming some of these issues and therefore remote sampling is likely to become more appropriate and better received in the future as a result. See page 173 for further details about how developing technology can assist in an EQA's work.

An external quality assurance parable

Once an EQA had planned out a remote sample and contacted the centre in plenty of time. The centre duly sent the information in a box to the EQA's home address on the allocated Friday. The EQA was working in her office upstairs when the courier arrived and she didn't hear the doorbell. When she went downstairs she found a card on the doormat saying that the courier had left the box with a neighbour. As she was in the middle of another piece of work she went back up to her office and determined to pick up the box from the neighbour later in the morning as she was planning to do the sample in the afternoon.

When she stopped work for lunch she went around to the neighbour's house and knocked on the door. She could see the box clearly through the frosted window of the neighbour's front door. There was no answer. Then she recalled that the neighbours had mentioned they were going to Brussels for a long weekend… they had left at lunchtime and would not be returning until late Monday night.

She already had commitments all day on Tuesday and Wednesday so she had to contact the centre and explain what had happened, then pick up the box and carry out the remote sample – following a full day's work – on Tuesday evening.

The moral of the story is get a louder doorbell – or ask couriers to always re-deliver items rather than leave them with neighbours.

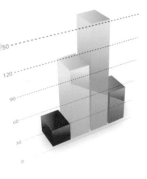

PLANNING A SYSTEMS VISIT [6312 unit 404 AC2.2 & AC 2.3]

In addition – or possibly as an alternative – to sampling the delivery of programmes/qualifications, the EQA may be planning to sample the overall systems used by the centre to support the delivery of all their programmes/qualifications. EQAs who monitor systems do not need and often do not have the technical knowledge of the programmes/qualifications that the centre delivers as it is not required in this role. However, the EQA has to have a thorough understanding of how systems operate in their own right and be knowledgeable, experienced and confident enough to identify issues and areas for development with senior managers in the centre. In the main, systems monitoring is done by longstanding EQAs who have undergone specific training for the role.

This systems sample is quite different to sampling learner work – for example, it can often involve centre staff who would not take part in a routine sampling visit, such as senior managers, quality managers, heads of departments, etc. It does not usually entail contact with learners at all. As the EQA's sample is one level removed from the IQA's sample, so the systems visit is one level more removed than a routine EQA visit.

The focus of systems monitoring is on the underpinning processes that the centre has in place to enable the delivery of learning rather than on *how* the learning is delivered. It looks at the processes the centre uses to manage programmes/qualifications, how they interact, the documentation that is maintained and often how the delivery of learning in the entire centre is managed.

The AO determines when a systems visit takes place and there are a range of reasons why this might be a priority.

Types of centres who might benefit from a systems visit include:
- an organisation that is applying to become a centre for the first time; if the centre has no experience of delivering accredited programmes/qualifications there are likely to be few systems in place
- an organisation that is already a centre with another AO and is applying for approval with a different AO
- an established centre whose managers feel they need to review where they currently are and are looking for guidance on how to improve their systems
- a centre that has emerged as a result of a merger, new partnership or consortium arrangement and is looking to have one overarching set of systems.

Not all AOs use this process. Find out if yours does by visiting their website.

Pre-approval systems visits

Often EQAs receive requests for systems visits because an organisation has applied to become a centre for the first time, and the AO has a policy of assisting new centres by discussing the required systems with them prior to an approval visit taking place.

In this situation the staff at the organisation may have very little knowledge about what systems need to be in place and may be starting with a 'blank sheet'. Most AOs have a range of support documents and training sessions that they will encourage the organisation to use to familiarise themselves with the requirements. The EQA may then be required at the initial systems visit to look at what the organisation already knows and has in place, help the team determine what they need to amend and identify new systems that they might need to develop and implement.

Often organisations that come forward to be centres are not familiar with the requirements for quality assurance in particular. They are usually knowledgeable about their technical/subject area, ie the vocational field in which they are going to deliver the programmes/qualifications. Centre staff will often have a grasp of how assessment works – even if only because they have been assessed themselves in the past – but may have no idea of other requirements, such as internal quality assurance. The systems visit can therefore be very useful in identifying what else the centre needs to introduce prior to seeking approval in their selected technical/subject area. The EQA will at this stage be able to guide and advise the centre about the best way to develop the necessary processes and documentation and help them to prepare for the approval process.

Systems visits to established centres

On an ongoing basis, AOs often require that a centre has a systems audit every year or every two years. This enables the AO to monitor that systems continue to meet the requirements, are used appropriately and that their application and effectiveness are reviewed regularly by the centre. It also enables the centre to be sure that what they are doing is appropriate, and provides an opportunity for them to ask the EQA for ideas about how to improve.

The underlying systems needed to be able to run a centre in general relate to:
- management
- resources
- candidate support
- assessment
- internal quality assurance
- continuous improvement
- record keeping.

So a visit to review systems would look at each of these areas in detail. The EQA would ask to examine documentation and records, then discuss how the systems work and how they could be improved with the centre staff.

The EQA would work in a methodical way through the above areas and also follow trails through the centre. So, for example, they might pick one cohort of learners and ask the centre to describe what has happened at every stage in relation to that cohort. They can then look at the systems that have been used from the time the programme/ qualification was started to its conclusion. This can be very useful in identifying gaps in systems.

In addition, the centre may have requested a review of their systems to ensure that they are still in compliance – particularly if the centre has had a period of great change.

When planning a systems visit the EQA will carry out much of the same activities as when planning a routine monitoring visit, but there will be no request for information related to specific programme/ qualifications and no planning to sample learners' work.

A typical EQA plan to monitor the systems in a centre will request that the following details are made available during the day:

- **Management systems** – what meetings the centre will hold/ holds, what policies and procedures are in place related to Health and Safety, Equality, appeals, etc, and how they are reviewed. Records of any sub-contractor or partnership arrangements, satellites, assessment sites. That there is a communication strategy in place and in use. Who is responsible for management systems in the centre.
- **Resources** – what resources the centre can access. What HR systems the centre has in place – such as how it manages identifying, recruiting and supporting the staff who will deliver programmes. How requests for equipment, machinery, materials, etc, are processed. That CVs and copies of certificates are held for all staff, how CPD is identified, planned and managed.
- **Candidate support** – how staff members will assist learners to achieve, all related documents including individual development plans for learners, learner handbooks, induction programmes, assessment plans, reviews of progress, access to resources such as libraries, Virtual Learning Environments (VLEs), etc.
- **Assessment** – how the centre organises assessment, including how it manages materials, controls candidate tracking, maintains and stores assessment records.

ASSESSMENT

- **Internal quality assurance**– the QA policy and what rationale is used for sampling, how IQAs plan, sample and feedback on all programmes/qualifications delivered. IQA records of observing tutors and assessors working, standardisation activities carried out and meetings held. Who is responsible for overall quality assurance in the centre.
- **Continuous improvement**– details of how the centre will implement improvements every year. What annual systems are in place, such as carrying out training needs analyses or skillscans to check that staff continue to meet requirements. Information about how staff development is planned and managed. How quality development plans are implemented. Who is responsible for continuous improvement in the centre.
- **Record keeping** – what records the centre will maintain and how it will ensure confidentiality and security. Required records relating to all aspects of the centre – learners, staff, contractors, liaison with AO, etc. Who is responsible for administration and record keeping systems in the centre.

So the visit clearly has a different purpose and focus, and therefore the planning required is also different. As outlined above, only very experienced EQAs undertake systems visits and many EQAs will not take part in them at all.

PLANNING FOR AN ADVISORY VISIT

[6312 unit 404 AC2.2 & AC 2.3]

An advisory visit is one where the focus of the day (or half day) is to give guidance to the centre on what they need to develop or how they can improve in order to meet the requirements of the programme or qualification. Sometimes advisory visits are requested because there has been a change in the team at a centre, or a change in the requirements of the programme/qualification, or because a problem has been identified and the centre needs support in order to work out how to rectify it, or simply because the centre has lost focus and managers feel the need for a new impetus in how they deliver a programme or qualification. These visits are carried out by an EQA or a technical expert in that particular programme or qualification.

Not all AOs use this process. Find out if yours does by visiting their website.

Whoever carries out the visit, it can take many different forms in response to the needs of the centre at that particular time.

ACTIVITY

List some activities that you think an EQA might carry out when advising a centre.

Your list may have included some of the following:
- holding discussions with various team members
- having discussions with managers
- making presentations
- holding question and answer sessions
- running a standardisation activity
- working through the requirements of a whole programme/ qualification with a team
- leading a meeting
- leading a standardisation activity
- delivering a training session
- assisting the centre to develop materials.

It is clear that these are very different activities to what is usually referred to as an EQA visit. In some instances an advisory visit may be carried out by a person who is not allocated to that centre at all. A good example of this is where the centre needs support in improving their assessment or internal quality assurance processes. The AO may request that an EQA who specialises in these areas carries out the visit and provides specific advice, rather than an EQA who works with the centre in a particular vocational area.

As a result of these fundamental differences, the planning that takes place is also very different and may take a number of forms. The advisory visit plan might be:
- informal and agreed by phone
- informal and agreed by email
- separately agreed and the methods prescribed by the AO
- carried out using the AO's usual documentation
- guided by the requirements of the programme/qualification.

But whatever the purpose or style of the advisory visit, the EQA will still agree what is to be done with the centre and the appropriate AO contact. Then they will plan what they are going to cover, gather information and prepare any materials and resources they may need.

CARRYING OUT A ROUTINE EXTERNAL QUALITY ASSURANCE VISIT [6312 unit 404 AC3.2]

As described in the previous sections, EQAs complete an entire planning process in readiness for carrying out a visit. Following this, the EQA then carries out the visit as agreed.

Routine visits can be carried out in a range of ways – this will often depend on the type of programme or qualification that is being sampled. Also, the design of the programme/qualification will determine which sampling methods the EQA has to use. For example, it may not be possible to observe practice – particularly if the programme/qualification does not require the demonstration of competence. Some programmes/qualifications are very short, so it is difficult to make a visit where interviews of learners can take place (other than interviews of those who have already completed). Or there may be very high numbers of learners undertaking a range of levels within a range of qualifications, so the EQA might decide that sampling of learner work at each level on each qualification is their focus rather than using other techniques.

However, all visits should contain certain activities in order to make effective use of the available time and to cover all the requirements. Most can take place at any point in the day.

ACTIVITY

What does the EQA need to do as part of the visit? Outline some of the practical actions that you think they may need to take.

Here are a couple of ideas to help you:
1   Prepare and save the report they will use to a memory stick before the visit.
2   At the start of the day hold an opening meeting with the team.

Hopefully your answer contained some of the following activities – and here is some additional information about the purpose of each:

EQA activity	Purpose
Prepare and save the report to a memory stick or other device before the visit	Save time and ensure EQA looks prepared and professional to centre staff.
At the start of the day hold an opening meeting with the team	For the EQA to inform the centre about any changes to requirements, developments, events, etc, and to answer any urgent queries. To find out about any changes at the centre. To agree: • when during the visit the learner interviews will take place • when new staff can meet the EQA • the time, location and participants in the observation • any changes to the original plan.
Commence report	To ensure that EQA accurately records what is said and what is found as the visit progresses.
Meet/interview new team members – record who, what they said	To check: • they can meet the requirements as stated in the programme/qualification specification • CVs and original or endorsed copies of relevant certificates • they have been inducted, issued with suitable materials and been supported into the team.
Sample learner work – record who, what, where, etc	To monitor: • how the learning has taken place • that learners have been registered promptly with the AO • that all the programme/qualification requirements have been met • that appropriate people have carried out the various roles • that assessment and internal quality assurance requirements have been met • that assessment practice and decisions are accurate and consistent across units, assessors, learners, sites, etc. To accurately record what was found.
Meet/interview learners – record who, what they said	To check that: • what was said by staff and found in learner records is accurate • they have been inducted and know about the appeals procedure • they have no concerns or queries that the AO should be aware of • their needs have been met • no policies or legislation have been breached • their opinions have been listened to during their time on the programme. To record a summary of what was said.

EQA activity	Purpose
Observe IQA observing assessor working with learners (may be at a different site) – record what was observed, who, what, where, etc	To ensure that IQA is: • carrying out accurate observations of team members • giving appropriate feedback to tutors and assessors. To record a summary of what was seen.
Review documents, plans, records and other centre materials – record what has been reviewed.	To check that: • documents and materials are up to date and accurate • systems are being used • actions described verbally are taking place • records are being maintained • reviews of policies, people and systems are taking place. To accurately record what was seen.
Give specific feedback to individual IQAs on what has been sampled.	To ensure that IQAs: • have detailed feedback about what has been sampled and found • understand what is acceptable, good and unacceptable practice • are clear about what they should be doing from here onwards.
At the end of the day hold a 'closing' meeting.	To ensure that all team members and managers: • understand what has been found and changes that need to be implemented • are fully aware of what the report contains • are clear about any action points required by anyone • have a chance to ask any remaining questions.

It is the EQA's responsibility to lead and manage the visit so it is up to them to ensure that good use is made of the time available. They need to be confident at the end of the visit that they have carried out a representative sample and seen enough to make recommendations to the AO, such as about releasing certificates or recommending that the centre be given DCS.

In order not to disrupt the centre's normal work, the EQA may need to be flexible in what they carry out when during the visit. However, for obvious reasons, the centre cannot be allowed to divert the EQA far from their plan for the day. [6317 unit 404 AC2.4]

So an EQA's typical visit *plan* might look something like this:

10am	Arrive and set up laptop
	Start report
	Hold opening meeting with team members and managers
11am	Meet new staff
	Examine CVs and original or endorsed copies of certificates
11.30am	Sample learner work
	Working lunch (!)
1pm	Interview learners
2pm	Observe IQA observing assessor working with learner
3pm	Sample documents, minutes of meetings, CPD records, standardisation records, etc
4pm	Hold closing meeting – read out content of report
	Answer any remaining questions
4.30pm	Pack up and leave

However, EQAs also have to be flexible and be prepared to alter their plan to accommodate the needs of centre staff and learners on the day of the visit. Often centre staff and learners have other commitments during the course of the day so in reality visits may be more fluid than the plan implies. It is never the intention that the EQA sampling process should inconvenience people or even stop the centre from functioning. In addition, unforeseen, unpredictable events and the plans of other people in the centre can have an impact. The EQA has to be able to adjust what they were expecting to do during the visit but maintain control to ensure that they get the maximum from the day.

The EQA can do this by clarifying at the opening meeting what is actually possible to do during the day and confirming the best way to achieve this. They can then try to accommodate the needs of others but still to a degree direct what happens at what times. If they feel that they are being 'herded' in a particular direction in order to deflect them from something, then they can simply revert to the original plan or agree further changes with the centre.

So, for example, if the EQA is told at the opening meeting that the planned observation is to take place 40 miles from the main base and will therefore take around three hours in total to carry out, they can request that the people who were going to be observed travel to the main base to carry out the activity (if this is feasible), ask to observe someone else or they may decide not to carry out the observation at all. In this situation they might phone the staff involved and note on the report why the observation did not take place and that it will definitely be part of the next visit.

Even when nothing major arises, in many cases visits *actually* run something like this:

10am	Arrive and set up laptop
	Start report
	Hold opening meeting with team members and managers
	Review progress on action points set at previous visit
	Sample some documents, minutes of meetings, CPD records, standardisation records, etc, as server is being closed for maintenance from 11am to 3.30pm
11am	Interview learners who need to leave by 11.30am
	Meet new staff
	Examine CVs and original or endorsed copies of new staff certificates
11.30am	Travel to assessment site
	Observe IQA observing assessor working with learner
	Return travel to main site, give IQA feedback
1pm	Sample learner work
	Working lunch (if very lucky!)
1.30pm	Interview learners by phone
	Sample learner work
3.45pm	Sample remaining documents, minutes of meetings, CPD records, standardisation records, etc
4.15pm	Hold closing meeting – read out content of report, agree action points and timescales
	Answer any remaining questions
4.45pm	Pack up and leave

It must always be the EQA, in negotiation with the centre, who determines what happens during the visit, ensures that nothing is missed and that they have gathered sufficient information to be confident in their recommendations to the AO.

The order in which the elements of the visit take place is really irrelevant as long as the most important actions have been carried out:

- systems and records have been examined
- discussions have been held with staff
- learners have been interviewed
- an observation has been carried out
- feedback has been given
- the report has been (mainly) completed.

The centre knows what met the requirements, what didn't, what they have to do to implement improvements and by when. They also know what the report will contain.

EXTERNAL QUALITY ASSURANCE TECHNIQUES [6312 unit 404 AC3.3]

As we saw in the previous sections, and as in the IQA role, there are a range of techniques that the EQA can use when carrying out a sample. Over a period of time an EQA will plan to use all the appropriate techniques outlined below in each centre in order to be sure that they are getting a truly representative picture of how the programmes or qualifications are being delivered.

They will usually have identified which primary techniques they will be using at each visit during the planning stage – for example, if they are going to hold discussions with learners or observe an IQA giving feedback to an assessor.

ACTIVITY

Most of the sampling techniques that an EQA would use have already been mentioned in 'EQA visit planning' (see page 119). How many can you recall and do you know of any others?

The combination of techniques that an EQA might select will depend on what they are focusing on during the visit and which ones are appropriate to the programme/qualification that they are sampling. Hopefully you will have included at least some of the techniques in the diagram below in your answer to the activity.

The techniques most often used by EQAs are:

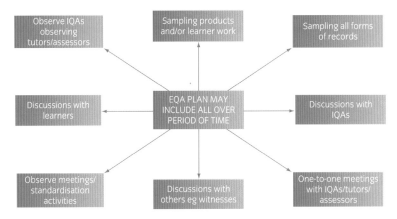

As with most options, there are benefits and disadvantages to each of the techniques, and some work better than others in certain situations – for example, although examining the record of a standardisation activity is useful, it is far better (whenever possible) to observe it taking place. However, the practical realities of trying to select a date when the EQA is available, the centre is ready for a visit and a standardisation activity is being held can cause problems. It is quite simply very difficult to co-ordinate all the people involved in such an activity. (It is considerably easier if the IQA has a support plan in place and standardisation is forward planned on an annual basis.) However, with perseverance it can be done and can be a very useful form of sampling.

There are a range of uses and potential pitfalls with each of the techniques. Here is a summary of the main ones:

Technique	Provides an opportunity to...	Some issues with each technique...
Sampling products/learner work	• make sure that all programme/ qualification requirements are met • check assessment and internal quality assurance processes • check all signatures and dates are in order • examine roles of all involved.	• can be time consuming • centres do not always provide the requested work.
Sampling records – paper and electronic	• make sure that records meet the requirements • follow audit trails • ensure adequate copies are kept • check storage, security and access.	• must not overtake other techniques and absorb all available time.

Technique	Provides an opportunity to...	Some issues with each technique...
Discussions with IQAs	• discuss around issues that have arisen • find out about reality of internal quality assurance at the centre • discuss issues arising from assessment practice • make suggestions about improving internal quality assurance • answer queries.	• takes time to gain trust • IQAs sometimes say what EQA wants to hear • IQA sometimes pursuing another agenda and trying to use EQAs to promote this.
One-to-one meetings with IQAs, tutors and assessors	• hold confidential conversations if needed • explore issues individuals may have • check individual's knowledge and understanding of requirements and systems • cross check against what others have said.	• can be perceived as threatening to management • staff sometimes say what EQA wants to hear • staff not always available • learners could be 'briefed' about what to say.
Discussions with others, eg witnesses	• discuss further what the witness has said about the learner • extend the EQA's understanding of how the programme actually works • discuss the ongoing support the centre provides to the learner and others.	• can be time consuming • witnesses can be intimidated by EQA role.
Observe meeting/ standardisation activity	• observe the interaction between team members • observe the way the IQA 'leads' the session • check consistency of understanding between team members • check the level and understanding of standardisation itself • make suggestions about other methods of standardisation • give feedback on activity observed.	• possibility of 'staged' interaction • EQA can take over activity • EQA can undermine IQA.
Discussions with learners	• discover the reality of how the programme/qualification has been delivered • explore the support they have received • talk about their work • uncover any areas of concern or dissatisfaction • cross check against what staff have said.	• learners not always available • learners sometimes intimidated by EQA role • learners could be 'briefed' about what to say.

Technique	Provides an opportunity to...	Some issues with each technique...
Observe IQA working with/ observing assessors	• see the process live • observe the preparation both parties carry out • listen to the feedback and guidance the IQA gives • observe the relationship between the IQA and the assessor • watch the record keeping carried out by both parties • gain useful additional information from sites away from main centre.	• time consuming – particularly if observation includes travel to sites away from main centre • often observation of assessment rather than IQA practice • can be used to deflect EQA from using other techniques.

When planning a routine visit, the EQA will select techniques that best suit what they are focusing on at the visit and that particular set of programmes/qualifications. In addition, EQAs will try to use techniques that they have not used with the centre before, which enable them to cover all of CAMERA and are appropriate to the vocational area.

There may also be specific sampling activities that are a requirement of the programme or qualification. For example, on some teaching qualifications there is a requirement that the EQA must carry out an observation of teaching practice at least once every year. Therefore the EQA for those qualifications will need to ensure that they meet this requirement by including observations in their plan and sample using this technique at least once every 12 months. So some techniques are specified in the programme or qualification guidance, and whatever technique the EQA carries out must always meet these requirements.

Most EQAs will quickly identify which techniques work best in certain situations with particular centres and plan their sampling accordingly. They are most likely to use a combination of techniques – it would be unusual to use only one technique at a visit. It is also useful to remember that when considering the techniques – or combination of techniques – that they will use on a visit, the EQA will be thinking about what they have done on past visits and planning to use as many as possible over a series of visits or a period of years.

So even if all the techniques are acceptable and appropriate in a particular centre, it may take three or more visits before the full range is used. In addition, what the EQA does during a visit and when they use the various techniques may be directly influenced by other developments or changes in the centre.

For example, in a centre over a three-year period the following may happen:

What happens	Techniques used at visit
May 2010 Centre is stable – routine visit	Observation of IQA and assessment practice, examine work products, interview learners, examine records
Jan 2011 Centre merges with another centre – routine visit	Discussions with new team members and managers, consideration of new arrangements, examine work products, examine records
May 2011 Revised qualifications launched – advisory visit	Discussions with team members and managers, explore plans, give guidance, review revised documents
Dec 2011 Centre is stable – early routine visit as no DCS on revised qualifications	Discuss experience and progress on new qualificationss, observe standardisation activity, examine work products, records, interview learners, examine records
June 2012 Centre is stable – remote sample	Examine work products, phone interviews of learners and witnesses, examine records
April 2013 Centre is stable - systems review visit	Examine and discuss whole centre systems, processes, records
June 2013 Centre is stable – routine visit	Observation of IQA and assessment practice, examining work products, interview learners, examine records

In most cases EQAs use more than one technique at each visit or sample.

So which techniques are used at particular times may be related to a range of factors and in response to changes in the centre. The EQA will be trained and supported by AO staff as they learn the most appropriate ones to select for each sample.

HOW EACH TECHNIQUE WORKS

Sampling all forms of records
This requires the EQA to look at a variety of documentation to see that IQAs, tutors and assessors are maintaining required records; that IQAs are sampling as planned, feedback is being given to assessors and any necessary action is being identified. Records can identify if learner progress is being tracked, standardisation is taking place, etc.

How it's done

This involves the EQA examining the records that the IQA, tutor and assessor have been completing, and monitoring the quality of the content. These records may be electronic and paper and may not all be in one location. The EQA will need to look at IQA sample plans, sampling records, feedback to assessors, minutes of meetings, notes from standardisation activities, staff CVs, CPD plans and records, logs of appeals, etc. The EQA may also consider learner records to confirm that they are making progress – they will check that all the specified records are maintained, all documents are up to date, stored appropriately and that the content and detail of the records is of a good standard and meets the requirements.

Discussions with IQAs

This is a very useful starting point for gaining information about how a centre's internal quality assurance works. It is also a way of gaining reassurance that the IQA understands what they are doing and why, and that they are committed to carrying out the role in a meaningful way. It can help the EQA to confirm that sampling, monitoring and developments are being carried out and that issues are being addressed. It can also provide an opportunity for the IQA to ask questions, access information and air concerns.

How it's done

The EQA requests that the IQA meet with them, and then asks the IQA to explain how the internal quality assurance processes work in the centre. The EQA will ask the IQA to show them the documents they use and to describe how they are used. The EQA will then look for these documents in the other materials that they sample – such as feedback from the IQA in assessor records.

One-to-one meetings with IQAs/tutors/assessors

This may be to look in detail at the work completed by a team member to explore actions and decisions taken. It may be related to a specific action, or because the team member is new, or just to check information provided by others. It also allows the staff member and EQA to discuss confidential or sensitive issues in private. In addition, it allows the EQA to cross check information provided by others.

How it's done

The EQA requests that the team member meet them – or, conversely, the staff member may request the meeting. These meetings can cover any topics that either party wishes to discuss but, unless otherwise agreed, the EQA should keep a summary record of what was discussed and what actions (if any) are to be taken by whom and by when. EQAs need to be very careful and sensitive to what is going on in a centre when having one-to-one meetings with team members. It could cause difficulties if the EQA was deemed to be interfering in the management of a centre or taking sides in a dispute. In addition, the EQA needs to be very clear about the areas of the discussion that they can report back to the centre management and the AO to be certain that they do not breach a confidence. It is useful to remember here that the EQA can only *make recommendations* about what the centre or individuals should do and report these recommendations back to the AO. It is the AO who makes the decisions about what actions the centre needs to take – based on the recommendations made by the EQA.

Discussions with others, eg witnesses

This is a very useful technique for gaining additional information about a learner and indeed about assessor practice. It is also a way of gaining reassurance about the integrity of the work that learners are completing. It can give a different perspective on how the team are performing with colleagues and other contributors to the programme/qualification.

How it's done

When sampling work products, the EQA can identify where others have made contributions to a learner's work, such as an employer. This would usually be in the form of a statement from a witness confirming the competent performance or the skills and abilities of the learner. Where witness statements are used, the learner should have included contact details for the witnesses in their work. The EQA asks the IQA if it is possible to make contact with the witness to ask them about the statements. The EQA can then ask appropriate open and probing questions to explore what the learner has done, how they have been supported, how often they have been visited, how clear the learner has been about what they should be doing next, etc. The EQA keeps rough notes of what the person says and includes a brief summary in their report. In some instances the EQA may later discuss what the person reported with the IQA and/or assessor.

Observe meetings and/or standardisation

These provide an opportunity for the EQA to see the IQA interacting with their team, and in particular to see the IQA leading an activity.

The EQA may be able to gauge the understanding of individual team members about the programme/qualifications they are delivering and gain an insight into the overall team understanding of standardisation.

How it's done

If the IQA produces an annual support plan (see page 68 for an example plan), then it is easy for the EQA to plan their visit to coincide with a team meeting or standardisation activity. As with most meetings, if they are planned well in advance then more people are likely to be able to attend. The EQA can agree with the IQA that they will contribute to the meeting or standardisation activity, or they might agree just to observe and take no active part. They will, however, answer queries if the IQA asks them to respond. In addition, the EQA can attend in order to facilitate the meeting or activity – this would then be likely to be part of an advisory visit (see page 131 for further details). Whatever is agreed the EQA will take notes and give feedback to the IQA after the meeting or activity is finished.

Discussions with learners

As mentioned previously, 'The proof of the pudding is in the eating' is a very true saying, and so sometimes to really find out about the quality of the work being delivered it is most effective to talk directly to the consumers of that work. Learners will often tell the EQA (as an objective third party) things that they would not divulge to their IQA, tutor or assessor. They should be able to provide information on why issues have arisen, why target dates have been missed and give detailed feedback about the support they are receiving – or not, as the case may be. There are some things that the EQA will need to keep in mind, however – for example, what they will do with any information that the learner may be sharing with them, how confidential it needs to be, whether it has any safety or other legislative implications – and thereafter use this information accordingly. The EQA will also need to use their judgement about the veracity of the information and be sensitive to any underlying motives or issues that may exist.

How it's done

In a similar way to the discussions with others, this needs to be thought through and recorded by the EQA. Though it may need to be managed in a sensitive and informal manner, this is another legitimate, formal sampling process. It needs to be treated as such, as in addition to the quality assurance function it may form part of other formal processes in the future. It requires that the EQA arranges to meet the learners with a series of prepared questions to prompt the discussion. Where learners lack confidence it can be better to carry out the discussions in a group – especially if they have been attending sessions together. However, sometimes – and on some qualifications – it works best when carried out one to one with the learner. A summary of what the learner says should be recorded – even if only in skeleton notes. Then, with the learner's permission, these can be discussed with others – including their IQA, tutor or assessor.

Observe IQAs observing assessors

This can be used by the EQA to monitor the interaction and rapport between the IQA and other team members. It is particularly useful for the EQA to observe the IQA giving feedback to an assessor following an observation of the assessor working with a learner.

It enables the EQA to see the IQA carrying out the process in a systematic way, to confirm that they are completing the required documentation – and that this is the same documentation that has been seen in use in other internal quality assurance processes. Also it allows the EQA to ensure that the IQA gives appropriate feedback (See page 63 for information on IQA feedback) and that they agree suitable forward action plans with the tutor or assessor.

How it's done

The EQA may have an outline checklist of what they are expecting to see during the observation, which could be based on the content of the appropriate IQA unit from the Training, Assessment and Quality Assurance (TAQA) suite (See Appendix 9 for an example of an EQA checklist). Failing that, the EQA would keep notes of what they observe. Following the observation they would start the feedback to the IQA by asking them how they thought the observation had gone and then talk through everything they had recorded on their checklist or in their notes. It is very important that the EQA gives good-quality feedback to the IQA, as IQAs will often use this as an example of best practice and base their feedback to their tutor/assessors on their own experiences.

Sampling products and/or learner work

The EQA uses this technique to ensure that learners are making expected progress, that they are producing what is required by the programme or qualification, that their work is valid, that the assessment decisions taken about the work are accurate, that the feedback being given about the work is appropriate and helpful, and that any necessary further development has been planned. In addition they will particularly look at the IQA sampling that has taken place and monitor the feedback that the IQA has given the tutor/assessor.

How it's done

Various centres have different issues with the practicalities of getting work in from learners, tutors and assessors in order for the EQA to carry out their planned sample. However – once again you can be sure that everything that can go wrong – does!

When the EQA plan includes sampling products – and most do – then near the date for the EQA visit the IQA needs to request the candidate's work and records from the tutor or assessor and prepare the paperwork. This might include producing checklists and feedback forms, checking the IQA plan, booking a room, etc, in readiness for the EQA visit. Then the IQA will also need to ensure that the requested learner's work, records and documents are in the same location as the EQA and held securely – this is far more difficult to achieve than it sounds on paper!

This sampling technique is where the EQA looks at what the candidate has produced and what decision and feedback they have been given by their tutor/assessor in relation to that work. They then check that the requirements of the programme or qualification have been met. The EQA then particularly looks at what sections of the assessor's work the IQA has sampled and the written feedback that the IQA has given to the assessor.

If this is an interim or formative sample of ongoing candidate work then the EQA will return the work to the IQA and give them feedback. The IQA will then pass this feedback on to the tutor/assessor.

If this is a final or summative sample of competed candidate work where the centre does not have DCS, then the EQA may finally 'sign off' the work as ready for the certificate to be claimed. They will then sign and date to own the decision that they have taken and fill in any necessary documentation to inform the centre that a certificate can be claimed.

So there are a range of techniques that can be used, and EQAs quickly learn which to select in each situation and which combinations work best.

MAKING DECISIONS – EVALUATING QUALITY [6312 unit 404 AC3.1 & AC3.2]

This is perhaps the most difficult part of the external quality assurance process to describe. It brings together all the experience and knowledge that the EQA has gained in delivering the programmes themselves and focuses it on what the centre has done. The EQA needs to be confident that what they observe and are told in their sample meets the requirements and maintains the quality and integrity of what is being delivered.

The decision-making process mainly occurs during or following sampling, and obviously before feedback is given.

When sampling, the EQA may use documents provided by the AO – such as the observation checklists or an EQA report form. However, whichever style of report they use, they will follow the audit trail laid down by the IQA, who should have completed an interim and final sample of learners' work in any cohort. They will examine what they find and consider the quality of what the IQA has recorded and fed back to the assessor.

It is useful to recall at this point that the EQA has considerably less time and opportunity to sample in the centre than the IQA has. So the EQA is relying on the IQA to carry out a representative sample and to fulfil the requirements of their role. Therefore the EQA will expect the IQA to have held meetings, managed the processes involved, observed the assessors, held discussions with the learners, witnesses and others, sampled work and records, etc, on a regular basis. The EQA will look for confirmation of this monitoring when they examine records and talk to people so that they can have confidence that the small amount that they themselves can sample at the visit is representative of the regular and ongoing work being carried out on the programme/qualification at the centre.

The principle is then that if what is found in this sample meets the requirements, it is reasonable to assume that everything on the programme/qualification will meet them. Conversely, if what is found does not meet the requirements, then other parts of the programme will not either. This may result in the centre losing some of its rights – for example, to be able to claim certificates without an EQA sample taking place.

The EQA selects the sample and initially concentrates on following:

- the audit trail of the IQA from their sample plan through to what the IQA actually sampled and when
- what feedback they gave
- what actions the IQA subsequently took.

The EQA will also:

- consider the standardisation undertaken
- discuss what has been done with the IQA
- possibly hold discussions with the assessors
- often hold discussions with learners
- cross check what staff have said by exploring the same issues and posing similar questions to various people and comparing what they are told.

The EQA will then decide – based on the entirety of what they find in the sample – whether the programme/qualification that is being delivered:

- has been properly planned
- follows the syllabus/course outline
- is in line with requirements
- meets the learners' needs
- encourages learner participation
- demonstrates good practice
- has been evaluated
- has been suitably recorded.

In the same way, in relation to assessment the EQA will decide – based on what they find in the sample – whether assessment decisions are:

- properly planned
- based on judgements against criteria
- sound
- accurate
- based on VARCS (Valid, Authentic, Reliable, Current and Sufficient)
- fully recorded and include agreed further action if necessary
- in line with AO requirements
- demonstrating good practice.

At some point during the sampling processes the EQA will take decisions – but it is useful to remember that the EQA only *makes recommendations* to the AO. It is the AO who decides what is going to happen to a centre, based on the EQA report and feedback.

Although the process aims to be as objective as possible, the EQA bases their decisions on what they see and are told at the visit. This information is then analysed and compared against criteria and specifications, so the EQA's decision is inevitably subjective to a degree. In addition, the EQA's viewpoint is often influenced by their previous experience and knowledge of the centre and of the IQA(s) involved.

EVIDENCE-BASED DECISION MAKING

It is extremely important that the EQA can justify the decisions they take, whether about IQA processes, training or assessment delivered at a centre. It can be useful for the EQA to formulate in their mind what they would show and how they would explain the decision to someone other than the IQA, such as their AO contact or even a representative of the relevant regulator.

It is only by being able to justify what they have done and said that the EQA will be able to defend the decision if challenged. The justification also helps the centre to understand exactly what has not been met and what they might be able to do to put it right. It is also useful to remember at this point that any challenge may not arise immediately, and so once again it is vital that sufficiently detailed records are kept in order that decisions can be explained if a query should arise.

In a summative sample, the EQA's decision may be that the delivery team have made an error or omission and as a result the learner (who has been told that they had finished) has not fully completed the programme or met all the requirements. In this situation the EQA decision may result in the IQA having to return the work to the tutor or assessor, who in turn may have to return it to the learner and request further work from them. Therefore sometimes the challenge to the EQA decision may come from other team members or even learners, rather than the IQA.

On occasion the challenge may be raised some time later – for example, when the IQA relays the outcome of the sample to their line manager the issue will be taken up and the EQA or AO will be contacted. Once again, as long as the EQA is clear why they have made the decision and can explain the rationale, this generally satisfies the person raising the issue. Though they may not agree with the decision, they understand why it was taken.

If the AO agrees with the recommendation but the centre does not – and the challenge is difficult to resolve – the AO may send a different, more experienced or technically knowledgeable EQA to explore what the original EQA has said in their report. This second EQA may confirm what the original report said, they may have a different perspective and 'soften' what the original EQA has said, or they may disagree and create a different report with different recommendations on outcomes and actions.

Whatever the outcome of the second visit, the recommendations once again have to be confirmed by the AO. Most challenges do not recur following a visit from a technical specialist, as whatever the specialist finds at the visit will generally be accepted by the AO and the centre.

Sometimes an AO representative may override the recommendation of an EQA. As mentioned earlier, the decision on outcomes and actions that a centre may need to take are determined by the AO, not by the EQA. The EQA makes recommendations. In these situations the AO officer will usually discuss the reasons for any changes with the EQA and justify their decision. Whatever the EQA thinks, the AO takes the decision.

JUDGING QUALITY WHEN SAMPLING

At some point in the process of sampling at the centre the EQA will make a judgement about the 'quality' of what the IQA, tutor or assessor has done. On page 10 we looked briefly at quality – and it is difficult to pin down exactly what it is in relation to learning. Is it when learners achieve quickly, or is it when they learn a great deal? Is quality the reason why attendance levels are excellent in some centres – or is it because the learners need the qualification? For both the EQA and the IQA, quality is quite difficult to quantify on individual programmes, cohorts or qualifications.

As previously mentioned, for many people the definition is 'Getting it right – first time and every time,' or that something is 'fit for purpose', but often quality is much less tangible than these phrases imply. Quality in learning is even more difficult to quantify.

However, most EQAs – like most people – know when they have seen quality and clearly know when it is missing. It could be 'quality' provision when all the requirements are met and the team and learners feel that the programme or qualification has done exactly what they expected. It might be visible where a tutor has enthused a group of learners about a particular topic, and this has captured their interest, resulting in work that is of a much higher level than was expected. It could be where an IQA identified a problem with a particular unit, so organised a standardisation activity during which good ideas were generated and then disseminated by the IQA, who then carried out some additional sampling and can confirm that the issue with the unit is resolved.

If something meets or exceeds expectations and has additional beneficial features then surely it is an example of quality.

ACTIVITY

What does quality practice look like in your role? If you are already involved in IQA sampling, think about a time when your EQA commented on the good quality in your work/centre. What justification did the EQA give for saying that what they found was an example of quality?

Hopefully your EQA was able to give you specific feedback about what you and your colleagues had done well that resulted in their judgement that what you were doing demonstrated 'quality'.

Where an EQA identifies 'quality', they should then record this on their report and give feedback to the IQA, tutor or assessor acknowledging their work.

The EQA may identify that other systems or working practices in the centre could be amended to encourage or support others to improve the quality of their work. Though the EQA would record this in their report, it would be the IQA's responsibility to take these opportunities forward to others in the organisation, such as the QAC or Quality Manager, as recommendations for any changes to be made.

Similarly, if the EQA has identified that requirements have not been met – and 'quality' is not happening – the EQA would record the detail of their finding on their report, suggest actions to be taken and give feedback to the IQA, tutor or assessor. Once again the IQA may want to share the ideas for change or development with others in the team – including senior managers.

On occasion, an IQA will ask the EQA to inform the senior managers of areas that need to be changed and the recommended actions. This is sometimes because the IQA feels that the management team do not appreciate the importance of carrying out actions recommended by the EQA. There could be resource implications and the managers might need to be convinced of the need to commit to the changes – and the costs!

So 'quality' in learning is difficult to describe and quantify, but clear to see where it exists and when it is missing. When an EQA sees it they will record this on their report of the visit. Where it needs to be developed they will record what they find with comments on how it could be improved and recommended actions to be taken.

GIVING SUPPORT AND FEEDBACK

[6312 unit 404 AC4.3]

When an EQA is sampling – whether at a centre or on a remote basis – the three most important functions that they carry out are probably:
- ensuring compliance
- providing advice, guidance, information and support to centres
- giving feedback.

Much of the information in previous sections refers to ensuring compliance, so this section focuses on how the EQA gives guidance and support and how they give effective feedback.

GIVING ADVICE, GUIDANCE AND SUPPORT

Do you recall that on page 95 a change was described in how external quality assurance is carried out?

To summarise what was said – the change is towards giving guidance and support to centres to 'get it right' rather than focusing effort on finding out when things have gone wrong. As a number of centres have already said – 'Tell us what we should be doing – don't just come and tell us when we haven't done it!'

This change means that EQAs can spend time working with centres as well as monitoring what they do and ensuring compliance with requirements.

As we have already explored, this approach has a large number of benefits because it is:
- less punitive
- focused on developing quality
- more conciliatory
- increasingly developmental in tone

- more supportive
- positive
- less hierarchical
- more flexible.

The EQA can now legitimately assist centres to develop their provision and guide them on how to introduce improvements into their practice.

ACTIVITY

What kinds of areas do you think EQAs might give advice and guidance on?

The answer is – anything that relates to how the centre functions and how it delivers the programmes/qualifications. This might include how to develop more effective practice in:
- management processes and systems
- how to meet the AO requirements
- resources – including suitability of staff
- candidate support – including initial assessment and induction
- new programme/qualification requirements
- learning delivery
- assessment
- internal quality assurance
- continuous improvement processes
- record keeping and data management.

So in order to give good-quality advice and guidance, EQAs have to keep up to date with what is happening on a number of levels. They need to know about:
- what developments the AO has planned or are underway
- any imminent changes to the programme/qualifications being delivered
- best practice in assessment
- best practice in internal quality assurance
- current trends and developments in their vocational or subject area
- future opportunities in their vocational or subject area such as training, events or meetings
- best practice in external quality assurance
- what is happening in their sector in relation to areas such as funding and legislation.

However, it is also very important that EQAs understand the parameters of their role.

This can be quite tricky – for example, where a centre asks for guidance on dealing with a member of their staff. Although the EQA might give guidance about what qualifications or experience an applicant should have in order to join the team, or what CPD a team member should undertake, they cannot give a view on what action should be taken if a team member carried out poor practice. They may suggest that a person should be further developed and may even propose some specific activities that they could carry out, but it would be totally inappropriate and beyond their remit for the EQA to suggest any other actions such as discipline or dismissal.

As outlined above, the EQA role is to support, guide and advise in relation to the programmes and qualifications being delivered, but it is not to interfere in how a centre manages its HR or indeed any part of its business.

GIVING FEEDBACK [6312 unit 404 AC4.3]

One of the ways in which an EQA can most assist a centre to develop and improve is by giving the team members good-quality feedback following a sample. In this capacity the EQA needs to be clear, professional, firm but diplomatic, while ensuring that the message is received and understood by the centre team.

Feedback from EQAs should always be given verbally, and then summarised and confirmed in writing as soon as possible after the sample. In the course of a visit feedback is often given verbally on an ongoing basis throughout the day – and it can be difficult to recall all of it when drawing together the report. So it is very important to record what is seen, what happens and what is said throughout the visit and not leave it to the end of the day (which is often rushed anyway) when it can be difficult to remember.

The principles of giving good-quality feedback apply to EQAs too.

ACTIVITY

Think of experiences you have had in receiving feedback. What worked well and what didn't? Why?

There are usually features of positive and constructive feedback that are significantly missing when feedback is unhelpful. Is that what you have recorded? Read the text below and reflect on whether the content illustrates what made the feedback you described above 'good' and what was missing when it wasn't a good experience.

Whether as a result of a visit or a remote sample, constructive feedback from EQAs to centres needs to:

- identify good or best practice
- be part of the plan for the visit
- be specific, detailed and avoid generalisations
- be factual and aimed only at improving practice
- be phrased objectively to reduce the sense of it being personal opinion
- be clear and as positive as possible
- provide constructive criticism that praises the strengths and is honest and clear about areas where changes of practice are required
- provide specific advice on how the learning delivery, assessment and internal quality assurance practice could be developed and improved further
- highlight opportunities for CPD for tutors, assessors and IQAs.

As described above, on a visit the EQA will often give informal verbal feedback throughout the day, and this should be helpful to the centre as it means that there will be no 'nasty surprises' during the formal feedback at the closing meeting. However, it is important that even this informal feedback is captured on the report as otherwise it is likely to be forgotten or overlooked by all parties.

It is common at the closing meeting for EQAs to start by summarising what they have found and been told, and so check that that their impressions are accurate. The EQA will usually then work through the content of the report, reading it out point by point. This gives a further opportunity to give or repeat explanations, ask and respond to any remaining questions and to check that the recorded information is accurate.

As there should have been constant dialogue between the EQA and the centre team during the visit, the feedback at the end of the day and the discussion about the content of the report should only ever be about minor disagreements in phraseology or style. There should not be any major surprises for the centre staff during the closing meeting about what has been identified by the EQA and included in the report, as this would have been fed back to them during the course of the visit. As mentioned earlier, the EQA needs to be professional, firm and diplomatic at this point and, as described on page 150, they have to be able to fully justify what they have recorded. This justification is key to the way that the feedback is received by the centre team – and to the likelihood of the necessary changes being made following the visit.

If the information recorded on the report is accurate, detailed and reflects what has been found, said and agreed, then the report should prove to be a useful tool for reminding the qualification team of what they are doing well and what they need to do to improve practice and/or ensure future compliance.

At the next visit, the first thing the EQA does is check that the actions agreed during the previous sample (whether desk-based or a visit) have been carried out. If they have not, then this will usually raise the level of risk in the centre and may result in a change of their centre rating – for example, they may lose the right to claim certificates between EQA visits. This is described in the next section.

DEALING WITH ISSUES AND DISPUTES [6312 unit 404 AC4.4]

Depending on what issues arise, there are a range of ways in which an EQA might be involved in dealing with problems related to centres. What action the AO and indeed the EQA are themselves required to take depends on what the problem entails and how serious the matter proves to be.

WHAT HAPPENS IF A CENTRE DOES NOT MEET ALL THE REQUIREMENTS?

When an EQA finds areas in a centre that are not in compliance or that breach requirements – and possibly regulations – then they will recommend that action be taken by the AO to limit the activities that the centre can carry out without close supervision. They will give the centre an action plan, which will be time bound, and also suggest a date when the situation should be reviewed – usually 3–6 months from the date of the original sample.

The EQA would feed the information that they have gathered during the sample through to the AO using the required documentation – usually a report. From the EQA recommendations, possibly with the addition of a phone call and discussion about previous track record, the AO staff member will determine the risk level in the centre and record this on their internal system. They will also decide at this point what support will be offered to the centre and what the centre is allowed to do.

Most AOs have a risk rating process that enables EQAs and AO staff to categorise a centre and establish the type and level of support that the centre might need.

The level of risk may result in the offer of different kinds of support from the AO to assist the centre to put right the areas that need improvement. Typically it might look like this:

Category of risk	What this means:	Type of support that AO might offer:
Low	• centre is allowed to register learners and claim certificates without an EQA having to complete a sample of learner work prior to the claim.	• routine system audit • routine EQA visit • network meetings for centre staff.
Medium	• centre is allowed to register learners but cannot claim certificates until an EQA has sampled learner work.	• early system visit • early EQA visit • advisory visit • interim remote sample • training for centre staff.
High	• centre is not allowed to register learners or claim certificates – this can also lead to the withdrawal of approval for some or all qualifications in a centre and can ultimately result in the AO withdrawing centre status altogether.	• investigation and meeting with centre management • early system visit • early EQA visit • advisory visit • training for centre staff.

So the decision on the risk rating of the centre is one taken by the AO but with consideration given to the outcome of the most recent EQA sample. The AO representative will also take the track record of the centre into account and any experience they may have had – or know of – related to the centre in the past.

It is impossible to be certain about what support an AO may put in place in any centre on any given qualification. Depending on the level of risk, the AO will determine what would be most helpful and effective for the centre. So, for example, in a centre that had always been reliable and had not given cause for concern in the past, a new IQAC has taken over in the previous six months and in a recent sample the EQA has found that some requirements are not being completed – depending on the level of seriousness in what they have found, the AO would be likely to keep the centre on a low risk rating but may decide that it would be worth arranging an early EQA visit back to the centre. The focus of the visit might be specifically to look at the areas found to be omitted at the last visit and might be a half-day in duration. Alternatively, if the issue was related to a specific area of a qualification, then the AO might decide to send in a technical expert in that area to carry out an advisory visit and to report back to the AO and previous EQA.

WHAT HAPPENS WHEN MALPRACTICE IS SUSPECTED?

Problems with centres can differ in how serious they are and therefore in the response that the AO needs to make. To reiterate – they are categorised by the risk they pose, so the AO might consider them to be low-, medium- or high-risk issues. The kind of action that the AO might take in relation to low-to-medium risks has been described above.

However, there are some areas of concern that would bring the full force of the AO's regulatory power into play. Typically this happens if the centre was carrying out actions where the:

- integrity of the programme or qualification was in question
- learners were being disadvantaged
- activity aroused suspicion of malpractice or even fraud.

EQAs must report malpractice immediately to the AO. The AO will advise the EQA what to do or say to the centre.

In these sorts of cases the AO would act quickly to limit what the centre would be allowed to do. As described above, the AO would be likely to block all new learner registrations and claims for certification made by the centre. It is likely then that the AO would arrange for a formal investigation to take place.

Whatever action is taken, the risk level is not likely to be amended until the agreed action has been satisfactorily completed.

Where the issue was one of suspected malpractice or fraud, the AO would be likely to:

- immediately remove the centre's approval to register learners and claim certificates
- refer the matter to their internal malpractice or investigation team
- keep the impending investigation confidential – the centre would not be informed that it was planned.

The EQA would be likely to be kept informed up to the point where the issue was referred to the malpractice/investigation team. From that point the issue would become confidential. However, the investigation team might ask the EQA to provide a statement about what they found and they would be likely to be informed of the outcome of the process once it was entirely complete.

ACTIVITY

Each AO has a well-established process for handling cases of suspected malpractice or fraud. Access and read the procedure from the AO with whom you have most contact.

In particular, look at the role and involvement of the EQA in the process.

THE EQA ROLE IN INTERNAL DISPUTES IN A CENTRE [6312 unit 404 AC4.4]

In addition to being involved in issues that they have identified when carrying out a sample of work in a centre, EQAs also occasionally get involved in assisting centres to resolve internal disputes.

Every centre delivering accredited programmes and/or qualifications has to have an appeals process (see Appendix 15) that they issue in a suitably accessible format to their learners. This means that the learners are aware of how to go about appealing against an assessment decision and know whom they need to communicate with if they were to disagree with a decision taken by their assessor.

In addition, centres are encouraged to have a complaints process that they also issue to learners. This process should be designed so that learners are able to lodge a complaint or raise an issue that is not an appeal against an assessment decision.

It is unusual for an EQA to become involved in such a complaint unless it was related to assessment or internal quality assurance practice and their opinion was requested. As this opinion or 'view' would be given on behalf of the AO, the EQA could not provide it to the centre unless they had previously discussed it with the AO and had been given specific permission to go ahead.

If an appeal is raised by a learner, it may be that the EQA is simply informed by the centre that the appeal is taking place and its outcome, and they would then pass this information on to the AO.

However, in some appeals processes EQAs may also be asked to give a technical opinion on the assessment decision. This would need to be agreed with the AO in advance and would often be completed by the EQA carrying out a remote sample of the assessment decision. They may also review other related assessment decisions by the same and other assessors in order to consider consistency – as they would in any other remote sample.

Also, on rare occasions, an EQA can be asked to take part in formal deliberations, such as an investigation or a hearing during the appeal. An EQA would never agree to carry out any of these activities without holding a full discussion with the AO, and then only if relevant AO staff were fully aware of the situation and what is going to happen and had given their express agreement.

To sum up – as EQAs are technical representatives of the AO, they are only in a position to report what they see, find and are told during a sample, and they can only make recommendations to the AO. This 'technical advice' role really only continues to a limited degree into any disputes that may arise. Before the EQA does anything else, having considered the issue they must suggest possible ways forward to the AO. Then, if the AO staff agree, the EQA can pass the suggestions on to the centre or take part in other activities designed to resolve the issue. But it is important to keep in mind that when a dispute has arisen the EQA cannot take *any* action or give *any* guidance without prior agreement and guidance from the AO.

INFORMATION MANAGEMENT IN THE EQA ROLE [6312 unit 404 AC5.1]

Record everything you say and do with a centre.

It is clear from previous chapters that the administration responsibilities in the EQA role rely on good organisational, planning and recording skills. An EQA has to be sensitive to the need for confidentiality and information security and has to be able to easily provide information on request from representatives of the AO.

All EQAs should be familiar with the requirements of the Data Protection Act (see page 81) and, in following the AO procedures for managing information, must protect the information that they hold about individual learners and staff. They will in turn talk to centres about maintaining this control over their own information.

There are fairly strict rules in place about how long information has to be stored, and in addition organisations like AOs often have specific internal requirements. However, as most storage systems are now electronic this is no longer the burden that it was in the past.

INFORMATION RELATED TO CENTRES

EQAs are required to keep copies of all the documents that they use related to a centre at least until they carry out the next activity. In many cases EQAs maintain documents for much longer periods than actually required, because they may use them as reference points for future activity.

As a minimum, for each centre an EQA would hold:
- contact details
- plans from previous visits and remote samples
- reports produced as a result of visits or remote samples
- emails to and from the centre
- emails to and from the AO related to the centre.

In addition, centre staff may also have sent to the EQA:

- CVs of additional staff whom the centre intend to add to their team
- CVs of staff about whom the centre has requested that the EQA give 'a view' as to whether they meet the requirements for a particular qualification
- documents that the centre has asked the EQA to review and comment on – such as their updated internal quality assurance procedures.

So the EQA needs to have a storage system that keeps this type of centre data safe and secure but easily accessible. This is important, as the EQA needs to be able to respond promptly to requests for information from the AO.

INFORMATION FROM THE AO

EQAs will also hold a great deal of information that has been provided by the AO. This is likely to include documents such as contact details for colleagues in the AO, materials related to the qualifications that they are quality assuring (such as assessment strategies, handbooks, logbooks, etc) and internal updates and newsletters.

Although this information may not be confidential in the way that personal details are, it should still be held 'commercially in confidence'. In other words, the AO would not expect this information to be forwarded or made available to centres, to external people or other organisations without the express permission of the AO itself.

Information from the AO may also include more sensitive information such as:

- updates on internal developments
- details of new or potential products (such as qualifications or publications)
- market intelligence
- future plans (such as for marketing, developing into new sectors, etc)
- risk assessments of specific centres
- any sensitive details relating to individual centres (such as problems they might be experiencing).

It is very important that the EQA appreciates the sensitivity of this information and stores it in a suitably secure place.

In a similar vein, information provided to EQAs by centres is very often held 'commercially in confidence'. Although the centre staff know that the information will be shared within the AO, they would not expect it to be accessible to or shared with anyone else.

OTHER INFORMATION HELD BY EQAS

In addition, an EQA is required to store and easily access information about themselves and their EQA work. For example, they may need to keep a record of the time they spend working; they will probably have a system for claiming and reconciling receipt of payments for their work with the AO and for maintaining their own CVs and CPD records.

RISKS WITH EQA INFORMATION

As you might imagine, all the risks that can affect information in general apply to the information held by EQAs. These are the typical risks:

- irretrievable loss of data, eg in a fire
- temporary loss of data, eg in a USB drive failure
- insecurity of systems – where information is accessible to unauthorised people
- information shared or used for purposes other than that for which it was intended and without the permission of relevant people
- ineffective or only partial destruction of obsolete or sensitive information – this could result in a breach of security.

Transporting information probably poses the biggest risk for an EQA. Whether the EQA is sending sensitive data by email or land mail, or is travelling with a laptop and memory stick, taking information away from the EQA's home base significantly increases the risk of a breach of security.

In relation to risks with information – assess all the probable and improbable risks, and expect the unlikely.

ACTIVITY

Identify some of the areas of risk that EQAs may have in relation to information security.

These are recent examples of some of the major pitfalls experienced by EQAs while transporting information:

- email with centre report attached sent to wrong centre with similar name
- learner's work (being returned to centre following a remote sample) lost by courier – and never recovered
- laptop left on the train
- laptop stolen from boot of car
- USB drive containing reports from a number of centres left plugged into a PC at a centre – and never recovered.

In some of these cases the EQA had to inform the centre(s) concerned. Although people are understanding, it also caused a great deal of disquiet and some friction among those involved.

Although it is difficult to cover all eventualities, here are some common sense points for transporting information:

1 Have the information backed-up at home/in the office
2 Double-check what has been attached to emails and where it is going before clicking 'Send'
3 Use recorded delivery and get receipts for all remittances sent by land mail – though this did not help in the example cited above
4 Pack up belongings in plenty of time before disembarking from public transport
5 Keep belongings close when travelling
6 Don't plug USB drives into other people's computers!

EFFECTIVE RECORDING PRACTICE

[6312 unit 404 AC5.1]

Always write reports in the third person and as if the content might be read by an outside agency, such as Ofqual.

Good recording practice is extremely important in the EQA role. As a baseline, the EQA needs to make a sufficiently detailed and accurate summary record/report of:

- their plans
- observations during the sampling
- their findings
- what they are told
- conclusions they have drawn
- agreed action to be taken
- recommendations they are making as a result of what they have found.

ACTIVITY

What might the detail in an EQA report be used for?

There are a number of uses made of the detail on any EQA report and therefore a number of reasons why effective recording is so important:

- It is obviously important that these records can be understood and implemented by the centre staff following the sample, and that the content can be used to communicate with others – such as senior managers – in the centre.
- It is also important that the EQA can use the reporting document to recall what they saw and agreed on the previous visit or as a result of the previous remote sample. The EQA would then review progress at the next activity – which could be 12 or more months later.
- If the centre disagrees with the content of the report or decisions taken by the EQA they may appeal. Initially the AO response to this would be entirely based on the content of the EQA report.

- An objective third party – for example, an auditor or inspector from a funding body, the AO or a regulator – needs to be able to understand what was planned, what happened, what was found and, most importantly, what it was that resulted in the EQA making their recommendations and giving action points. Any resultant formal or informal investigation would start by focusing on the content of the report.
- On a regular basis the person who co-ordinates the work of the EQA on behalf of the AO will sample the content of reports to try to standardise how EQAs work and how they record their sampling across different sectors and geographical locations. It is much easier to do this when reports are detailed and specific with clear justifications recorded.
- The quality of reporting practice is one of the indicators on which EQA performance is judged. So it is in the EQA's own interest to provide full, detailed and specific records of their activities.

THE EQA REPORT [6312 unit 404 AC5.1]

Different AOs use different reporting documents with a variety of content. However, they all have some common requirements.

In general, EQA reports should include specific detail of the following:
- the name of the EQA
- the date of the activity
- what the activity consisted of
- the names and contact details of all relevant people
- the site visited
- the learner work sampled
- the records sampled
- whom the EQA met
- what sampling techniques they carried out, eg if they held a discussion with a learner, examined learner work or observed an assessment taking place
- what the EQA was shown and told about areas such as:
  - management systems
  - resources
  - learner support
  - assessment
  - internal quality assurance
  - continuous improvement
  - record keeping.

It is what is recorded on an EQA report that determines how the report can be used in the future. See page 116 for what the EQA looks for in relation to each of these items.

In order to ensure that they record suitable information in each section, the EQA would note something like the following:

But most importantly it is the *level of detail and quality* of what is recorded that makes a report useful or not.

Area	Record of having seen or been told about…
Management systems	• policies that are in place and when they were last or are due to be reviewed • any updates on changes to the centre • whether notification of changes has been sent to AO and EQA • sufficient suitable number of tutors, assessors and IQAs in place • an up-to-date written set of internal quality assurance procedures • records related to satellite centres or consortia arrangements • how candidate records and work are stored • communication between team members, eg dates of minutes of meetings, dates of records of standardisation.
Resources	• sufficiency of staff resources and any changes • how staff records are kept – list of CVs, certificates, development plans and CPD seen in sample • how staff are inducted into teams and information is available to them • Health and Safety policies and how they are communicated • insurance • sufficiency and suitability of equipment • use of Realistic Work Environments (RWE) • any Recognition of Prior Learning (RPL) undertaken • details of discussions held with team members – who and a brief summary of what was said.
Learner support	• learner induction pack seen in use • details of learner development and assessment plans seen • issues of access to assessment • the appeals procedure and how it is communicated to learners • details of initial assessments completed – by when, for whom and how they are used • details of discussions with learners – who and a brief summary of what was said.
Assessment	• relevant and up-to-date versions of qualification specs being used • outline of assessment documentation sampled (if not recorded elsewhere) including suitability of plans and records of assessment • details of tracking system of learner progress • brief description of observation of assessment undertaken – who, what, where, when, etc • brief description of acceptable assessment methods used/not used • details of feedback sampled – written and during observation (if done).

Area	Record of having seen or been told about...
Internal quality assurance	• how centre understands and implements internal quality assurance processes • up-to-date AO documents being used • how sampling is planned and stored • different sampling techniques used, eg examining records, discussions with learners, discussions with witnesses, observation of IQA and assessor practice • quality of feedback to assessors • records of IQA observations of assessors • evidence and quality of standardisation taking place • how CPD and assessor performance is monitored.
Continuous improvement	• annual TNA or competence checks being carried out on IQAs and assessors • current quality development plan for centre or department • CPD plans and records for staff • how previous action plans having been implemented • how and when policies have been reviewed • evaluation feedback from all parties – including learners – on how it is used to improve programmes.
Record keeping	• reviews of policies taking place • IQA plans, records, feedback to assessors, observation checklists • learner records – including registration details, all assessment documentation, tracking systems, evaluations • minutes of a variety of meetings and activities.

An external quality assurance report can be used for a range of purposes and can ultimately be the focus of an investigation. Therefore it is very important that relevant information is recorded about the required areas with a high level of detail. The fact that an EQA saw or was told about something during a visit is of little value – unless the EQA records that they sampled it or were told about it.

Each report should give the reader sufficient relevant information to be able to understand what the EQA saw and was told. This then forms the justification for the decisions taken, recommendations made and actions agreed. It should also clearly follow an internal quality assurance audit trail and lay an external audit trail that is clear to see. So it should be very simple to identify what the EQA sampled and therefore what they have based their decision(s) upon.

Many EQAs initial and date evidence in a colour – often green. This is simply to differentiate clearly that they have sampled the evidence, as opposed to assessors, who often initial in blue or black, and IQAs, who often use red.

Though this is not a regulatory requirement, it does mean that anyone carrying out any kind of inspection or investigation can use the report as the basis of the external quality assurance audit trail. They can look at what the EQA sampled, see their initial on the work itself and consider the decisions the EQA has taken about the work.

If an informal investigation has arisen because the centre simply does not agree with the EQA's decision and the outcome of the sample, then another EQA may be sent into the centre to sample exactly the same learner work. This is considerably easier to carry out if the report identifies the reference numbers and type of work sampled and the original EQA has initialled it in green. The second EQA would follow the audit trail and decide if they agree with the content of the original report, the decisions made, actions agreed and the recommendations put in place. This would then be reported back to the AO and decisions taken on what to do next.

A more formal investigation would carry out exactly the same process – the investigation team would follow what was recorded on the external quality assurance report(s) and look to see who initialled what work and when – often looking for inconsistencies.

As a result it is crucial that recording is accurate, complete and contains enough detail for the report to be used as a tool by a range of people – including the centre itself, the AO local team and possibly an investigation team.

As described in earlier sections, the content of all EQA reports should be an accurate, detailed, specific and full summary of what the EQA has seen, found and been told – with conclusions drawn and recommendations made to the AO.

Look at these paragraphs – they are anonymised genuine records from two different EQAs. In both cases nothing has been removed or added and they are both what the EQA recorded about the same area: management systems.

EQA One

The centre QAC has just completed the handover process to the new QAC, AD. The centre administration will be carried out by KS but other than that AD will manage the centre. The SCTC staff have now joined the centre team and all future SCTC learners will complete their qualifications through this centre. In April 2012 one member of the assessment team, JM, will be leaving and MS will be joining the team. The centre will need to forward a CU form regarding this. There will be two IQA team meetings in 2012 – April/ May and Oct/Nov followed by full team meetings. The new QAC will set the dates. Since August 2011 the centre has run Unit 605 programmes for internal staff and has evaluated how this has worked. There are plans for this process to continue but no set date for future programmes. On the unit 605 programme the team has evaluated with all parties involved. They report that it has been very interesting and a real learning process for all concerned – there are areas of the programme that will probably be changed as a result. Around 48 learners have been started via 5 workshops in Durham. Of these – around 20 have completed but none have yet been certificated as the centre did not have DCS. This is the first time the centre has delivered this unit to learners. The IQA procedures are all up to date with TAQA terminology throughout. Saw minutes of full team standardisation meeting on 29.10.11 and saw notes of focused standardisation activity producing a marking guide for Unit 609 assignment. Also saw minutes of IQA meeting on 27.09.11. Tracking of learners seems very well organised and all requested records were readily available before and during the visit.

EQA Two

The centre staff have adapted well to the management, delivery and assessment of the 7478-02 award. Good co-ordination between assessor and QA/IV.

The biggest difference between the two examples is in the level of detail recorded and the quality of the specific information that has been included.

From reading this single section completed by EQA One, it is clear what has been happening at the centre, the meetings and developments that have taken place, that the procedures are up to date and that standardisation is taking place. In addition the reader could be confident that the records and tracking systems are all up to date, accurate and available.

The statement from EQA Two says very little. It does not explain how the staff have adapted – there is no information on what the EQA was told about what the centre had done nor a description of what the EQA was shown.

ACTIVITY

Here are two more real-life examples for you to read but this time the EQAs have recorded comments about candidate support

EQA One
Once again good practice seen in candidate support. All portfolios had evidence of regular reviews carried out and progress and achievement logged. Very good quality assessment planning seen throughout – by the assessors and candidate-assessors. It is really gratifying seeing the candidate-assessors implementing the good practice they have seen carried out by their own assessors. Learners are encouraged to comment on their assessments and planning. They are very positive and clear about what they have done in relation to the unit and understand what they need to do next. The candidate interviewed face-to-face repeatedly expressed her gratitude to other IQAs and her mentor/countersigner (DJ) for the support they had given her during the time she had worked on V1. This excellent support was clear in the feedback he had given her on her IQA decisions – which were then included as Witness Testimonies in her portfolio. Both learners interviewed by phone also commented on the amount of and quality of the support they had had.

EQA Three
Feedback following the assessment is constructive, related and reflected the performance of the learners.

Again from reading just the one section written by EQA One you have a strong sense of the level of support that has been found in the candidate's work and then cross checked and confirmed verbally.

The comment by EQA Three does not tell you what the EQA found or how s/he found it. It can be assumed that they observed this happening but because so little detail has been recorded it is not clear on what they have based their judgement. In addition, candidate/learner support is much more than just receiving feedback, but EQA Three has not recorded anything else that the centre staff are doing to support their learners.

As well as the sense of what is said, the actual words and phrases used can also make a great deal of difference. They can clarify or obscure the message that the EQA is trying to get across. They can also assist or obstruct the centre's understanding of what they are being judged against and what they are required to do. It is important that the words are accurate and the phraseology is as objective as possible.

ACTIVITY

Consider these statements:

Statement One
'I am not happy with the way that the candidate's work is stored.'

Statement Two
'In the Centre Manual it states that candidate's work must be stored securely and access must be restricted to appropriate people. Assessors need to be made aware of this requirement and to follow the existing centre procedure.'

Statement Three
'I am less than satisfied with the way that assessment is being recorded.'

Statement Four
'Assessors must record the "who, what, where, when and how" of all assessments carried out. There is guidance in the Qualification Handbook about what has to be recorded, examples of best practice – and it contains useful forms for recording what takes place.'

Ignoring the lack of detail in Statements One and Three, what else can you note that is different between statements One and Two and between statements Three and Four?

See page 221 for answers.

The EQA role is to assist centres to understand and implement the requirements set by the regulators, occupational sector body and AO. It is not to set personal standards and arbitrarily apply them. It is important that EQAs understand that they are helping the centre to comply and are monitoring against the requirements set by the regulators, the occupational sector body and the AO – not by standards that they have set themselves.

So it is extremely important that what is recorded in the EQA report is in line with the set requirements, objective and factual, positive and supportive, and clearly expressed.

RECORDING THE SPECIFIC DETAIL OF THE LEARNER WORK SAMPLED

One area where it is crucial that the external quality assurance record contains sufficient detail is where actual pieces of learner work have been sampled.

The type of data that the EQA needs to record in relation to learner work is:
- learner name
- learner start date
- date of registration with the AO
- the name of the assessor
- the name of the IQA
- whether the work has been sampled by the IQA – and, if yes, when
- whether the learner has completed the requirements or is still making progress
- the work sampled by the EQA
- the different assessment methods sampled
- the EQA techniques used in the sample.

In terms of the audit trail, this is the sort of detail that an EQA needs to record in relation to what they have looked at in one candidate's work:

Learner One
Sampled portfolio – evidence of interim and final IQA sampling. Sampled reviews and assessment plans. Sampled unit 605 Evidence 12 & 13(OBS), 14(PD), 15(PE). Unit 601 Evidence 16(ASS). Interviewed candidate.

Learner Two
Sampled portfolio – evidence of interim IQA sampling. Interviewed candidate. Sampled unit 601 Evidence 1(OBS), 2(PD), 3(OBS), 7(PE), 5a(PE), 12(ASS). Incomplete portfolio.

Learner Three

Unit 603 sampled Assessment Plans, IQA records. Sampled portfolio Evidence 1(PE), 4(LS), 5(WQ), 6(WT), 7(OBS). Evidence of good reflective practice in PS. Interviewed candidate by phone.

Key to abbreviations:

OBS – record of an observation

PD – record of planned discussion

WQ – answers to written
      questions

LS – learner statement

PE – product evidence

ASS – assignment

WT – witness testimony

This level of detail is very important to create the audit trail and to make it clear to everyone what has been sampled – and therefore what the EQA's judgements and comments are based on.

Managing, recording, storing and transporting information are important functions of the EQA, and when information systems break down the outcome can be far reaching. If information is not held appropriately and securely there could potentially be breaches of procedures, regulations, confidentiality and data protection. This is definitely not a situation that any EQA would want to be involved in.

THE IMPACT OF TECHNOLOGY IN EQA INFORMATION MANAGEMENT [6312 unit 404

AC3.3 & AC6.2]

Since EQAs first started working for AOs they have used the technology of the time. Originally this would have been telephones, handwritten reports, photocopiers and the Royal Mail.

'Any sufficiently advanced technology is indistinguishable from magic.' Arthur C. Clarke

Currently EQAs mainly use the following in their role:
- electronic storage on a home or office computer
- laptops and tablet computers
- email
- phones – particularly mobiles
- e-portfolios
- forums
- websites – including that of their own AO
- webinars.

It is fair to say that at present EQAs are not fully capitalising on all available technology and many are wary of Information and Computer Technology (ICT) in general. As a community EQAs have been uncertain about ICT and in some cases reluctant to see the potential that it may have to support them in their role.

Technology can be used to enhance and ease the external quality assurance process – it can also be used to increase efficiency and save on travel time and costs. Centres often use and provide the following information electronically for the EQA prior to a visit or remote sample:

- staff data
- IQA sample plans
- learner tracking data.

So most EQAs have some experience of retrieving information from email attachments, viewing data on screen and responding by email prior to a visit or remote sample.

E-PORTFOLIOS

Some EQAs will also have experience of sampling e-portfolios to which they would have been granted remote access by the centre. The biggest concern that EQAs have with e-portfolios is that many versions are available and each one has different features, requirements and properties. As the EQA will probably only use a particular type of e-portfolio for a few days once each year, every time they access it feels like the first time they have ever seen the portfolio. This can cause most anxiety for the EQA when they are accessing the e-portfolio on a remote basis.

In addition, EQAs have the same concerns about e-portfolios that they have always had about paper-based versions. These concerns are typically about how the (e-)portfolio demonstrates the:

- authenticity of learner work
- support being provided to learners
- robustness of assessment
- quality of assessment planning, decision making, feedback and recording
- internal quality assurance sample planning
- audit trail of sampling and recording
- arrangements for countersigning of assessment (when required).

So EQAs are often wary of e-portfolios in general as they do not feel confident in accessing them, nor do they feel certain that the content of the e-portfolio can satisfy the requirements stipulated in any qualification or programme.

However, most AOs are encouraging centres to use e-portfolios and often they will recommend one particular version. This will mean that more EQAs will have greater exposure to a variety of e-portfolios in the coming years and, no doubt, as familiarity increases, anxiety will decrease.

LEARNER WORK STORED ELECTRONICALLY

Increasingly work produced by learners is stored electronically – whether these are in simple files such as Microsoft Word or Excel or in an all-singing-all-dancing e-portfolio. The types of learner work to be sampled by the EQA can vary greatly from scanned-in basic text through to:

- online interactive activities
- video clip evidence of skills/performance
- digitally recorded verbal evidence
- still photographic images.

In addition to using electronic planning and tracking records, centre staff might also electronically store:

- records of computer-based/online testing
- virtual standardisation activities – including webinars.

In addition, as part of their work EQAs might need to be able to use:

- collaborative technologies, such as telephone and video conferencing
- webinars.

Teleconferences and videoconferencing are both becoming more commonly used as organisations and individuals strive to be more efficient in their working. There are a number of particular drivers to this goal:

- cost effectiveness
- effective use of time
- attempts to reduce environmental impact.

For EQAs there are some concerns about the use of these alternatives to face-to-face contact. For example, a remote (or desk-based) sample carried out electronically can work well, but many EQAs fear that it can also mean less rigour in their monitoring of centres. In the main they are concerned that it is far more difficult to identify issues in a centre from a remote sample than it is during a visit.

Similarly, centres often comment that they don't like remote samples as the opportunity to learn from the EQA is lost, as is the opportunity to ask the questions that are not important enough to require separate contact with an EQA between visits.

As with all major changes to working practices there are various levels of acceptance of the new technologies amongst the EQA team. However, putting aside personal preferences, it is important that a sensible and reasonable balance is struck between actual face-to-face support and monitoring of centres and remote or electronic sampling.

The acceptance and use of technologies in external quality assurance will inevitably increase in the coming years. This is because the available electronic tools will become more refined and more accessible; more learners will demand online learning and support; EQAs will gain in confidence through familiarity and, most significantly, the next generation of EQAs will have used ICT throughout their entire school and work careers so they would not expect to use anything else.

Access your AO's website regularly to keep up to date with policy changes.

LEGAL ISSUES, POLICIES AND PROCEDURES [6312 unit 404 AC6.1]

See page 81 for a summary of the main requirements of the Data Protection Act and information about where to access details of relevant legislation.

Most EQAs carry out their role with little consideration of the legislation that they comply with each time they carry out their work. However, during their monitoring they are often required to comment on the ways in which the centres comply with the legislation and what policies and procedures they have in place to ensure compliance. They are also expected to promote best practice in relation to the legislation and to support centres to develop excellence in implementing the requirements.

As representatives of the AO, EQAs are bound by the policies and procedures that the organisation has put in place in order to ensure that they carry out best practice but also that they stay within the requirements of the legislation.

ACTIVITY

Visit www.direct.gov.uk and look at the summaries of the following areas of legislation, all of which may impact on the role of an EQA:
1   Data Protection and Confidentiality
2   Health and Safety
3   Equality and Diversity
4   Bilingualism
5   Age Discrimination

Having looked at the salient points of the legislation, how do you think they might affect the EQA in their day-to-day work? Which areas do you think would be of particular risk?

If you are already working as an EQA, you could check yourself against the summary points in the main pieces of legislation and think about any changes you may need to introduce into your working practices.

Note here actions that you could take in your work to ensure that you do not contravene the legislation and to enable you to actively promote best practice in centres.

1

2

3

4

5

As is the case with many work roles, often EQAs do not give a thought to the legislation related to their role – until a problem arises.

DATA PROTECTION AND CONFIDENTIALITY

[6312 unit 404 AC6.1]

As EQAs go about their daily work of organising, planning and preparing for visits they come into immediate contact with the legislation related to managing information that is inevitably sent over the internet. They must ensure that they do not breach the Data Protection Act and that they maintain confidentiality at all times (see also page 81).

In addition, when the EQA is carrying out a remote sample, the secure transport and storage of the learner and centre material is paramount, as outlined on page 164.

HEALTH AND SAFETY AT WORK [6312 unit 404 AC6.1]

When EQAs carry out visits they are responsible for their own safety and that of others. This is also the case when travelling to and from centres and when carrying out the visit at the centre premises.

So if they are visiting or carrying out an observation of a workplace where there are additional risks, such as hazardous materials or dangerous machinery, they must take additional precautions to stay safe – for example, by finding out about restricted areas, wearing appropriate Personal Protective Equipment (PPE) or ensuring that they know about emergency evacuation routes. Whatever is required – and even where there is no obvious risk – it is the EQA's own responsibility to ensure that they are at least compliant with the legislation and the procedures of the centre – or, preferably, that they model best practice in meeting Health and Safety requirements.

EQUALITY AND DIVERSITY [6312 unit 404 AC6.3]

All AOs have Equality and Diversity statements and policies. At the very least they will have an 'Access to Assessment' policy that ensures candidates are not discriminated against in their being able to be assessed. (Interestingly, it is night-shift workers who often feel that they do not have equal access to assessors, as assessors often work office hours, ie 9am to 5pm.)

It is very important that EQAs promote good practice in this area and that they model excellent practice in their behaviour, what they say and what they do while at a centre. EQAs must feel sufficiently confident to challenge poor practice that appears to be discriminatory if they are ever confronted by it. This means that they must be able to recognise it and know what to do. It is fair to say that most centres and many EQAs have an understanding of what constitutes poor practice in relation to equality issues – and it does not often arise as a specific issue – but they do not always know what to do when they are confronted by it.

ACTIVITY

What do you think an EQA should do if they suspect that a learner or group of learners is not being treated fairly and that the situation/arrangements/centre/lack of planning may be discriminating against them?

The initial action that an EQA should take in these sorts of situations is to immediately request guidance from their AO. The AO is likely to ask them to report their findings – depending on the situation – as this could be an issue of poor practice or even suspected malpractice. They may direct the EQA not to record the findings on the report that would also be sent to the centre, but to report the situation to them directly, eg in an email. The most important point here is that the EQA must not act unilaterally – they must get instruction from the AO before they do or say anything to the centre about the issue. The AO will then guide the EQA about what to do or say and then, if necessary, implement their procedures for dealing with poor practice or malpractice.

BILINGUALISM [6312 unit 404 AC6.3]

In the UK this directly applies to two languages only. These languages – Welsh and Irish – are deemed to have equal status with English, and this status has been protected by legislation. Separate guidance exists for speakers of any other languages in the UK.

The Welsh Language Act 1993 establishes in UK law the equality of the Welsh and English languages in Wales. It places an obligation on the public sector to treat the Welsh and English languages equally in the provision of services to the public in Wales.

In Northern Ireland in March 2001 the UK government ratified the European Charter for Regional or Minority Languages in relation to the use of Irish in Northern Ireland. The Charter seeks to safeguard and encourage the use of historical and minority languages throughout Europe.

REGULATORY REQUIREMENTS [6312 unit 404 AC1.4]

I addition to legislation, there are also areas of regulatory requirements that affect the EQA role (see also page 17).These regulations can be general – for example, they might apply to all qualifications of a particular type, such as those listed in the QCF – or they can relate only to one particular programme or qualification. An example of this would be the requirement for an EQA to carry out an observation of teaching practice at every sample. This is an example of a specific requirement in certain teaching qualifications and is the kind of obligation that the EQA has to ensure they carry out at every visit. Relevant EQAs would be very aware that they must fulfil the action as stated in the regulations.

In general, it is more likely that EQAs will consciously follow and implement regulatory requirements more than any others, as these would have been introduced to them when they delivered the programme themselves, or when they were initially informed about the qualification content. The requirements would be something that they would take into account at every sample and would be uppermost in their minds when they put together their plan for the sample.

ACTIVITY

Think about a qualification that you are familiar with. Are there any regulations relating to it that would affect the sampling carried out by an EQA?

POLICIES AND PROCEDURES [6312 unit 404 AC6.1]

Each AO has a range of policies and procedures in place that EQAs are required to comply with in their work. Some are directly related to EQA practice (like the need to send planning documents to centres within certain timescales) and have to be followed at all times.

Others have a more indirect impact, such as policies or procedures related to the operational requirements that exist in the AO, of which the EQA team may only be a small part.

ACTIVITY

Visit: www.cityandguilds.com

What policies does City & Guilds already have in place that directly relate to the EQA role?

See 221 page for answer.

Keeping up to date with regulations, legislation, policies and subject information is one of the most challenging areas of being an EQA – particularly when major changes are underway. The introduction of the QCF was a good example of this. As soon as the framework was definitely going ahead, centres started to ask their EQA for information. The AOs delivered introductory briefing events, sent out information, set up forums, developed specific pages on their websites related to the changes and made presentations at conferences. However, a major source of information for centres was their own EQA. It was really important that EQAs were fully informed about each stage of the introduction of the new framework and that they understood the way that this would impact on centres.

'By three methods we may learn wisdom: first, by reflection, which is noblest; second, by imitation, which is easiest; and third, by experience, which is the bitterest.' Confucius

It is a requirement of all EQAs that they keep up to date with the policies and procedures of the AO and that they are at the forefront of providing information when changes take place (for more details see page 183).

REFLECTIVE PRACTICE AND CPD

[6312 unit 404 AC6.4]

As described in Part 2: Internal quality assurance, in all professional practice and in all roles where responsibility is held in learning and development, there is a requirement for people to reflect on their decisions, actions and the resultant outcomes. They need to consider what they have done, identify if there were alternative courses of action that might have been more effective and learn from the experiences that they have had.

ACTIVITY

Think about an activity that you have recently carried out that involved you in monitoring work undertaken by other people and giving them feedback. (If you have done this for external people rather than colleagues then it will be more akin to the role of an EQA.) Think about it in detail, if possible break it down into steps and be brutally honest with yourself!

Consider:
- what went well
- what did not go to plan
- what you would do differently if you were required to do it again
- what you learned from the experience
- what you can do to improve your performance.

These sorts of questions are the basis of reflective practice, and they work well for EQAs. They can be applied to everyday occurrences in the workplace, specific tasks undertaken and one-off projects. They can also – if adapted slightly – be used when reflecting on learning activities.

As described in Part 2, reflective practice is said to be a process of considering or analysing experiences in order to learn from them, and is very much a feature of the principle of 'lifelong learning'. There are a wide range of models of reflection readily available on the internet. However, most follow the same overriding principle – that it is a useful activity that promotes learning and can result in demonstrable improvement to professional practice.

ACTIVITY

Look up at least three different models of reflection. Which one(s) best fits your style of reflective practice?

EQAs are encouraged to regularly reflect on their work, on experiences they have had, on learning activities and on information that they have gathered. By so doing they should be in a good position to improve their practice and develop the quality of their work in the role.

In addition the AO may expect that EQAs will complete some form of self-reflection and on occasion they will be asked to review their own performance annually prior to it being reviewed by the person/department in the AO who takes responsibility for the development of EQAs.

ACTIVITY

It would be a useful starting point in considering yourself in an EQA role to have a dispassionate look at yourself and itemise where in the role you feel that your Strengths, Development needs and Opportunities to develop lie.

EQA Activity	Strengths	Development needs	Opportunity to develop
Communication			
Planning			
Objectivity			
Diplomacy			
Managing self			
Analysing data			
Staying focused			
Being firm			
Giving feedback			
Reporting			

Prospective EQAs can use the outcome of such an analysis to identify their development needs and clarify possible areas where they need to develop their practice. The development needs could be recorded on a development or CPD plan (see Appendix 16) for the forthcoming period. The outcome of the analysis could also be used to form the basis of a discussion with someone (a mentor perhaps?) who may be able to give feedback and possibly put forward their opinion about what the analysis appears to indicate.

FEEDBACK AND REFLECTION

Once in an EQA role, in addition and in support of reflective practice, feedback from others can be extremely useful. In most AOs this feedback would be from the AO representative who is responsible for co-ordinating or monitoring the work of the EQA. They may be sampling the EQA's work on an ongoing basis and they may also undertake to accompany the EQA on a visit. This feedback can provide information, guidance and perspectives that can assist the EQA in considering areas where they need to develop skills, knowledge and understanding. These could then be recorded on the development or CPD plan, as outlined above.

In addition, sharing a reflection on an experience and requesting feedback from a trusted source can allow an EQA to explore difficult situations and might result in significant changes to the way that they then approach issues in the future. Many EQAs will discuss issues like this with colleague EQAs, relevant staff from the AO – or indeed the AO representative to whom they report.

Feedback can provide perspectives that may change an EQA's approach or working practices and so improve their ability and confidence in carrying out the role.

In most AOs, in addition to informal feedback there is likely to be regular formal feedback from the person who manages the EQA's work. For example, they or their work will be:
- sampled by an AO representative
- included in the content of AO reports
- monitored or supervised by a line manager or AO co-ordinator
- the subject of the AO's review process.

This type of feedback would usually be annual, following a review process, and given in relation to an agreed set of criteria or objectives that the person's work or performance had been 'judged' against. In most AOs the assessment criteria from the LLUK External Quality Assurance units (built out of NOS Standard 12 for Learning & Development 2010) is used as the criteria for EQA performance (see Appendix 20 for Standard 12). Inevitably, then, the feedback is likely to relate only to that criteria and is usually given in a formal way. This can obviously be useful but is perhaps not the most effective type of feedback for the EQA who is a regular reflective practitioner. They may benefit considerably more from the regular, less formal feedback provided by colleagues as a result of ongoing sampling and support.

CONTINUING PROFESSIONAL DEVELOPMENT (CPD) [6312 unit 404 AC6.4]

EQAs (as with IQAs) need to complete at least two types of CPD every year. They must keep their EQA practice up to date but they will also need to maintain the currency of their technical knowledge and experience related to the qualifications or programmes that they quality assure. Before an EQA takes any action on CPD, it is wise to check the AO guidance or strategy for the role and then to consider if there are any specific requirements in the programmes or qualifications that they are quality assuring. EQAs may need to provide evidence of keeping their CPD in line with requirements on an annual basis.

Keep up to date with what training your AO is offering centres. You might find it useful to attend.

There is one area of contention in relation to EQA practice and CPD. Because EQAs need to be experienced and mature practitioners, often they will continue to carry out the role following their retirement from employment. The role by its very nature is not full time and for people who are retired it is an attractive option. However, as stated above, an EQA needs to keep their technical experience up to date and this can be an issue for someone who is retired and no longer carries out any tutor/assessor/IQA role in their sector. This is more of an issue in some sectors where major changes are rapid and occur regularly (eg in ICT) and in sectors where external factors, such as fashion, may have a major impact (eg in hairdressing).

An EQA who has not been a practising hairdresser for over five years is not likely to have a great deal of technical experience in bonding hair extensions, for example. In such situations the EQA will sometimes organise to spend time working in a centre every year where they can at least bring their knowledge up to date and have some understanding of the emerging and new processes. This is extremely valuable CPD, as it ensures that they maintain their credibility in centres on an ongoing basis. However, not all EQAs are able to continue as practitioners – even on a one-off activity basis – and so it could be said that they are no longer able to keep their technical experience up to date.

However, they can still keep their technical knowledge and experience of external quality assurance up to date by attending AO events, actively carrying out the EQA role, reading recent literature, researching in the subject, etc.

As outlined above, an EQA may have an annual development or CPD plan (see Appendix 16) that they follow. This may be compiled as the result of a performance review carried out by the AO or from other activities that they have completed, for example self-reflection using a tool such as a SWOT analysis (see page 88), or other activity designed to identify development needs.

ACTIVITY [6317 unit 401 AC1.4]

Look at the assessment strategy or guidance provided in support of the programmes or qualifications that you would be most likely to externally quality assure. What CPD requirements do you think you would need to meet each year?

You will probably find that most programmes and qualifications do not identify specific CPD requirements for EQAs. It is the AOs who state what CPD activities their EQAs have to carry out every year. In most cases the AO will also deliver or arrange at least some of the events and activities that the EQAs are required to complete.

CPD activities can take many forms, and, as a model of good practice, EQAs should try to undertake a range of these in any given year. (Though, obviously, they must first and foremost carry out the activities required by their AO and/or any specification.)

The main CPD activities that EQAs might engage in include:
- requesting feedback
- undertaking training courses
- individual research
- attending forums
- completing related qualifications
- shadowing another EQA
- standardisation activities
- contributing to related consultations and surveys
- undertaking related reading
- attending relevant meetings or conferences
- developing qualifications
- developing materials in support of qualifications
- being observed.

As you may have realised, some of the activities are similar to those that are available to an IQA.

There are a wide range of tools available for storing CPD information – both electronic and on paper. A very important feature, however, is that this process should not be complicated and records should be easy to maintain. See Appendix 18 for an example of what a simple document for recording EQA CPD could contain.

In addition, some professional institutes and AOs have their own facilities for storing CPD records online.

Whatever form the processes of reflection, analysis, development planning and recording take, the focus for the EQA must always be on how this can:
- meet any stated requirements
- improve quality
- enhance professional practice
- increase efficiency and effectiveness.

SUMMARY

The following points were covered in Part 3: External quality assurance:

- what is external quality assurance?
- the most common model of external quality assurance
- the focus of external quality assurance
- the main functions of external quality assurance
- the role of the EQA
- qualities, skills and abilities needed by an EQA
- becoming an EQA – recruitment and induction
- responsibilities of an EQA
- the quality assurance starting point
- planning and preparation for EQA activities
- sample planning
- risk management
- carrying out a range of visits
- external quality assurance techniques
- making decisions – evaluating quality
- giving support and feedback
- dealing with issues and disputes
- information management in the EQA role
- effective recording practice
- the impact of technology in EQA information management
- legal issues, policies and procedures
- reflective practice and CPD.

APPENDIX 1: BOOKLIST

LEVEL 3 AND 4 AWARDS AND CERTIFICATES IN ASSESSMENT AND QUALITY ASSURANCE (6317): RECOMMENDED READING LIST

Brookfield, S. D. (1995) *Becoming a Critically Reflective Teacher,* San Francisco: Jossey-Bass

DfES (2004) *Planning Learning, Recording Progress and Reporting Achievement – a guide for practitioners*

Ecclestone, K. (2005, 2nd Edn) *Understanding Assessment and Qualifications in Post-Compulsory Education and Training*, Ashford: NIACE

Flood, A. et al, (2009) *Authenticity: A Guide for Teachers,* Coventry: Ofqual

Gravells, A. (2011, 2nd Edn) *Principles and Practice of Assessment in the Lifelong Learning Sector*, Exeter: Learning Matters

Gravells, A. and Simpson, S. (2009) *Equality and Diversity in the Lifelong Learning Sector,* Exeter: Learning Matters

Griffiths, M. and Tann, S. (1992) 'Using Reflective Practice to Link Personal and Public Theories', *Journal of Education for Teaching*, Vol. 18, No. 1, pp. 69–85

Hattie, J. and Timperley, H. (2007) 'The Power of Feedback', *Review of Educational Research*, Vol. 77, No. 1, pp. 81–112

QCA (2007) *Regulatory Principles for e-assessment,* London: Qualifications and Curriculum Authority

Race, P., Brown, S. and Smith, B. (2004) *500 Tips on Assessment*, Abingdon: Routledge

Schön, D. (1983) *The Reflective Practitioner*, New York: Basic Books

Schön, D. (1991) *The Reflective Practitioner: How Professionals Think in Action*, London: Farnham Ashgate Publishing Ltd

Tummons, J. (2007, 2nd Edn) *Assessing Learning in the Lifelong Learning Sector*, Exeter: Learning Matters

Wood, J. and Dickinson, J. (2011) *Quality Assurance and Evaluation in the Lifelong Learning Sector,* Exeter: Learning Matters

APPENDIX 2: USEFUL WEBSITES

LEVEL 3 AND 4 AWARDS AND CERTIFICATES IN ASSESSMENT AND QUALITY ASSURANCE (6317): RECOMMENDED WEBSITE LIST

Access to qualifications: http://wales.gov.uk/topics/educationandskills/qualificationsinwales/?lang=en

Assessment guidance booklets: www.sflip.org.uk/assessment/assessmentguidance.aspx

Assessment methods: www.brookes.ac.uk/services/ocsld/resources/methods.html

Education Scotland: www.hmie.gov.uk

City & Guilds: www.cityandguilds.com/uk-home.html

Chartered Institute of Educational Assessors: www.ciea.org.uk

Data Protection: www.direct.gov.uk

Department for Education and Skills (Wales Government) http://wales.gov.uk/topics/educationandskills/?skip=1&lang=en

Estyn Wales: www.estyn.gov.uk

ETI Northern Ireland: www.etini.gov.uk

Equality and Diversity Forum: www.edf.org.uk

Equality and Human Rights Commission: www.uk250.co.uk/frame/4060/disability-rights-commission.html

Government legislation: www.legislation.gov.uk

Legislation explained: www.direct.gov.uk

Health & Safety Executive: www.hse.gov.uk

Initial Assessment: www.excellencegateway.org.uk/page.aspx?o=barnsleymbcrarpa

Institute for Learning: www.ifl.ac.uk

Learning Styles: www.vark-learn.com

Learning and Skills Improvement Service (LSIS): www.excellencegateway.org.uk/node/57

Observations of teaching and learning: www.excellencegateway.org.uk/page.aspx?o=128948

Ofsted: www.ofsted.gov.uk

Peer and self-assessment: www.nclrc.org/essentials/assessing/peereval.htm

Plagiarism: www.plagiarism.org

Plagiarism checker: www.plagiarismchecker.com

Qualifications and Credit Framework: www.qcda.gov.uk/qualifications/60.aspx

RARPA: www.ladder4learning.org.uk/resources/learning/rarpa

Reflective practice: www.learningandteaching.info/learning/reflecti.htm

Sector Skills Councils: www.sscalliance.org

Skills Development Scotland: www.skillsdevelopmentscotland.co.uk

APPENDIX 3: GLOSSARY

AO	Awarding Organisation
Authentic	Being the learner's own work
Assessment	A process of measuring the achievement of learners
CCEA	Council for Curriculum, Examinations and Assessment (regulator – Northern Ireland)
Competence	The ability to complete tasks to set standards or criteria
Compliance	Meeting requirements
CPD	Continuing Professional Development, the continuing process of acquiring experience, skills and knowledge throughout work and life
DfES	Department for Education and Skills, Welsh Government (regulator – Wales)
Diversity	Acknowledging that each individual is unique and recognising our individual differences in, for example, culture, ability, gender, race, religion, wealth, sexual orientation, or any other individual characteristic
EQA	External Quality Assurer
Equality	A state of fair treatment that is the right of all people regardless of differences in, for example, culture, ability, gender, race, religion, wealth, sexual orientation, or any other group characteristic
ESTYN	Welsh Government Inspection Service
ETI	Education and Training Inspectorate – Northern Ireland
Fair	Ensuring that everyone has an equal chance of getting an objective and accurate assessment
Feedback	Written or verbal information given to others regarding their performance and practice
HMIE	Her Majesty's Inspectorate of Education (now part of 'Education Scotland')
IQA	Internal Quality Assurer
Ofqual	Office of Qualifications and Exam Regulation (regulator – England)
Ofsted	Office for Standards in Education, Children's Services and Skills – England
QAC	Quality Assurance Co-ordinator
QCF	Qualifications and Credit Framework
Quality assurance	Internal and external systems and procedures for monitoring the assessment process and ensuring the reliability of assessment decisions
Reliable	Consistently achieves the same results with different assessors and the same (or similar) group of learners
Requirements	These could be the requirements of the practitioner's own organisation or those of an external organisation, such as an AO
Sectors	Occupational areas, such as hairdressing or construction
SDS	Skills Development Scotland

SQA	Scottish Qualifications Authority
SSB	Standards Setting Bodies
SSC	Sector Skills Councils
Standardisation	Activities undertaken to promote, develop and ensure consistency, eg between assessors
TNA	Training Needs Analysis
Valid	Relevant to the criteria being assessed
VARCS	Valid, Authentic, Reliable, Current and Sufficient

APPENDIX 4: EXAMPLE INTERNAL QUALITY ASSURANCE STRATEGY

This shows the kinds of information that centres may include in their internal quality assurance strategy. The appendix might contain links to the electronic documents that team members have to use when carrying out their roles. The following are extracts Sections 6 and 7 from the strategy whose contents list is below. The documents referred to in brackets in the following sections have not been included as they are currently in use in the centre.

	CONTENTS
	Index
1	Introduction
2	Centre Structure and Roles
3	Qualification Delivery
4	Quality Assurance of Qualification Delivery
5	Qualification Assessment
6	Verification of Assessment
7	Monitoring of Assessment Practice
8	Procedure for Developing and Supporting Centre Team Members, assessors and Internal Quality Assurers.
Appendix 1	Centre Documents List

Sections 6 and 7 of the above IQA Strategy

Section 6. Verification of Assessment

6.1 The aim of verifying assessment is to ensure consistency and reliability of assessment and internal quality assurance decisions. This applies to all learners registered with the Centre. The verification process will include the Learner Journey and the initial assessment process.

6.2 All learners registered with the Centre will have equal access to assessment and verification. The process has been outlined in the QCF/NVQ Flowchart (DC1) and the QCF/VRQ Flowchart (DC2) (forms referred to in this document are not included).

6.3 The methods of verifying assessments are:
- sampling assessments – learner portfolios (SC 2)
- monitoring assessment practice (SC 3)
- standardising assessment judgements
- standardising marking of assignments.

6.4 The IQA carries out interim and final verification of portfolios on a planned sample basis (SC 2). All IQA samples are recorded. Feedback is provided to the assessor in both written and verbal formats as soon as is practical after the verification (SC 14).

6.5 The rationale for the sampling process is outlined in the IQA Sampling Strategy (SC 4).

6.6 The IQAC monitors assessment practice to ensure that all assessors adhere to the Awarding Organisation standards of assessment and the Centre's Assessment Policy.

6.7 The IQAC must ensure that learners are aware of and satisfied with this process. During Induction, all registered learners are provided with the procedures for Complaints and Appeals (SC 5 & 6), statements regarding Equal Opportunities and Welsh Language (QAC 7 & 11) and notices regarding Data Protection, Confidentiality and Plagiarism (SC 8/9/10). These are reiterated during qualifications and before each assessment opportunity. The IQAC will apply and monitor both the Centre's and the Awarding Organisation Equal Opportunities Policy and access procedures through the assessment process.

6.8 Assessment is monitored and constructive feedback is recorded by the methods highlighted in the Assessment Monitoring Strategy (SC 12).

6.9 The IQAC/IQAs standardise assessment judgements to ensure that each assessor consistently makes valid decisions over time and with different learners (SC 2 & 14).

6.10 For NVQs all assessors are monitored to ensure that a sufficient number make the same decision on the same evidence base. The IQAC/IQAs may have to check different assessment sites to ensure assessment decisions are consistent (SC 2 & 16).

6.11 Standardisation meetings are organised at least bi-annually and more often when new qualifications are being introduced. The standardisation meetings involve the IQAC, IQAs and assessors. Depending on the qualification, standardisation activities may include:

- collating copies of evidence presented for one unit and asking the team to make a decision based on what is in front of them
- concentrating on a particular type of evidence and how it is assessed including recording
- peer observations and feedback (SC 3)
- developing written questions and model answers
- reading and marking assignments
- consideration of each other's assessment decisions.
- looking at models of good practice.

Section 7. Monitoring of Assessment Practice

7.1 The IQAC monitors assessment practice to ensure that all assessors adhere to national standards of assessment and to ensure that learners are aware of and satisfied with this process. The Centre has developed an Assessment Monitoring Strategy (SC 12).

7.2 All assessors are monitored to ensure that a sufficient number make the same decision on the same evidence. This monitoring may be by colleagues or peers in the qualification team but in addition the IQAC must monitor and give feedback to the assessor using the following methods as relevant to the qualification:

- observation of performance
- reviewing of assessment records
- verifying portfolios
- verifying assignment marking
- verifying feedback to learners
- gathering feedback from learners
- one-to-one supervision
- standardisation activities.

7.3 The IQAC standardises assessment judgements to ensure that each assessor consistently makes valid decisions over time and with different learners. The IQAC also standardises to ensure that all assessors working on the qualification are making consistent judgements across the team.

7.4 Assessors are required to take part in and contribute to standardisation activities organised by the IQAC for their programme.

7.5 Assessors are required to attend meetings convened by the IQAC for their programme that may include:

- meetings with the EQA
- meetings with commissioning customers
- team meetings to review learner achievement and progress
- team meetings to plan and review qualification and Centre development
- standardisation meetings
- team development activities.

7.6 A qualified member of the team will validate and countersign all assessment or verification decisions for learner assessor or IQAs (SC 21).

7.7 The IQAC will increase the level of sampling and monitoring of assessment practice for new team members (whether qualified or not) learner assessor and IQAs. The IQAC will also increase the level of sampling if learners have submitted a complaint or an appeal, or if there are discrepancies with the assessors' judgements.

7.8 Each learner will complete an interim (SC 30) and final evaluation (SC 31) on assessor and Centre performance. It is the responsibility of the Programme Coordinators to ensure that evaluation sheet are sent out, monitored and collated and that the results are fed back to IQAC and assessors.

APPENDIX 5: IQA OBSERVATION CHECKLIST I
TUTOR FACILITATING LEARNING TO GROUPS (L&D UNIT 8)

IQA Name: _____ Date: _____

Tutor Name: _____ Qual: _____

Unit 8 Assessment Criteria Did the tutor...	Y/N	How it was demonstrated
2.1 Clarify which facilitation methods they would use with group members to meet group and individual learning objectives?		
2.2 Implement learning and development activities to meet learning objectives?		
2.3 Manage risks to the group and individual's learning and development?		
1.1 Develop opportunities for individuals to apply new knowledge and skills in practical contexts?		
1.2 Provide feedback to improve the application of the learning?		
a. Support self-evaluation by learners?		
b. Review individual responses to learning and development in groups?		
c. Assist learners to identify their future learning and development needs?		
Feedback and comments		
Action agreed		**By when**

IQA signature _____

Date _____

Tutor signature _____

Date _____

APPENDIX 6: IQA OBSERVATION CHECKLIST II

TUTOR FACILITATING LEARNING FOR INDIVIDUALS (L&D UNIT 9)

IQA Name: _____   Date: _____

Tutor Name: _____   Qual: _____

Unit 9 Assessment Criteria Did the tutor....	Y/N	How it was demonstrated
2.1 Clarify which facilitation methods they would use with individuals to meet their learning and/or development objectives?		
2.2 Implement activities to meet learning and/or development objectives?		
2.3 Manage risks and safeguard learners participating in one-to-one learning and/or development?		
3.1 Develop opportunities for individuals to apply their new knowledge and learning in practical contexts?		
1.1 Explain the benefits of self-evaluation to individuals?		
1.2 Review individual responses to one-to-one learning and/or development?		
1.3 Assist individual learners to identify their future learning and/or development needs?		
Feedback and comments		
Action agreed		By when

IQA signature _____

Date _____

Tutor signature _____

Date _____

APPENDIX 7: IQA OBSERVATION CHECKLIST III
ASSESSOR ASSESSING COMPETENCE (TAQA UNIT 302)

IQA Name: _____   Date: _____

Tutor Name: _____   Qual: _____

Unit 302 Assessment Criteria Did the trainee assessor...	Y/N	How it was demonstrated
1.1 Plan the assessment of occupational competence?		
1.2 Communicate the purpose, requirements and processes of assessing occupational competence to the learner?		
1.3 Plan the assessment of occupational competence to address learner needs and current achievements?		
1.4 Identify opportunities for holistic assessment?		
2.1 Use valid, fair and reliable assessment methods?		
2.2 Make assessment decisions of occupational competence against specified criteria?		
2.3 Follow standardisation procedures?		
2.4 Provide feedback to learners which affirms achievement and identifies any further implications for learning, assessment and progression?		
3.1 Maintain records of the assessment of occupational competence, its outcomes and learner progress?		
4.1 Follow relevant policies, procedures and legislation for the assessment of occupational competence including those for health, safety and welfare?		

Unit 302 Assessment Criteria Did the trainee assessor...	Y/N	How it was demonstrated
4.2 Apply requirements for equality and diversity and, where appropriate, bilingualism when assessing occupational competence?		
1.4 Evaluate own work in carrying out assessments of occupational competence?		
Feedback and comments		
Action agreed		**By when**

IQA signature _____

Date _____

Tutor signature _____

Date _____

APPENDIX 8: IQA OBSERVATION CHECKLIST IV

ASSESSOR ASSESSING VOC SKILLS, K&U (TAQA UNIT 303)

IQA Name: _____   Date: _____

Tutor Name: _____   Qual: _____

Unit 303 Assessment Criteria Did the trainee assessor....	Y/N	How it was demonstrated
1.1 Select methods to assess vocational skills, knowledge and understanding which address learner needs and meet assessment requirements?		
1.2 Prepare resources and conditions for the assessment of vocational skills, knowledge and understanding?		
1.3 Communicate the purpose, requirements and processes of assessment of vocational skills, knowledge and understanding to learners?		
2.1 Manage assessments of vocational skills, knowledge and understanding to meet assessment requirements?		
2.2 Provide support to learners within agreed limitations?		
2.3 Analyse evidence of learner achievement?		
2.4 Make assessment decisions relating to vocational skills, knowledge and understanding against specified criteria?		
2.5 Provide feedback to the learner that affirms achievement and any further implications for learning, assessment and progression?		
2.6 Provide feedback to learners that affirms achievement and outline any further learning or assessment?		
3.1 Maintain records of the assessment of vocational skills, knowledge and understanding, its outcomes and learner progress?		
3.2 Follow procedures for the confidentiality of assessment information?		

Unit 303 Assessment Criteria Did the trainee assessor....	Y/N	How it was demonstrated
4.1 Follow relevant policies, procedures and legislation relating to the assessment of vocational skills, knowledge and understanding, including those for health, safety and welfare?		
4.2 Apply requirements for equality and diversity and, where appropriate, bilingualism?		
4.3 Evaluate own work in carrying out assessments of vocational skills, knowledge and understanding?		
Feedback and comments		
Action agreed		**By when**

IQA signature _____

Date _____

Tutor signature _____

Date _____

APPENDIX 9: EQA OBSERVATION CHECKLIST

IQA OBSERVING ASSESSOR (BASED ON TAQA UNIT 402)

EQA Name: _____ Date: _____

IQA Name: _____ Assessor Initials: _____

Based on Unit 402 Did the IQA.....	Y/N	How it was demonstrated
1. Have the observation recorded on their IQA plan?		
2. Agree the time and location for the observation of the assessor?		
3. Communicate the purpose, requirements and processes of observation to the assessor?		
4. Provide support to the assessor within appropriate limitations?		
5. Check the assessment decision?		
6. Provide feedback to the assessor that affirmed good practice and identified any actions required?		
7. Give feedback that was specific about strengths and weaknesses in terms of the quality of planning, interaction with learners, observations, assessment decisions and records?		
8. Give constructive criticism which praised the strengths and was honest and clear about areas where changes of practice were required?		
9. Give feedback that highlighted opportunities for Continuing Professional Development (CPD) for the assessor?		
10. Maintain records of the observation, its outcome and any required actions		
11. Follow procedures for the confidentiality of information?		
12. Follow relevant policies, procedures and legislation, including those for health, safety and welfare?		
13. Apply requirements for equality and diversity and, where appropriate, bilingualism?		
14. Evaluate their own work in carrying out the observation of assessor?		
Feedback and comments		
Action agreed		**By when**

EQA signature _____

Date _____

IQA signature _____

Date _____

APPENDIX 10: TYPICAL PROGRAMME TEAM MEETING AGENDA

CHAIR IQA: AB   **Circulation**   **Tutors:** CD & EF

Date: _____   **Assessors:** GH, JK, LM & NO

Time: _____

Location: _____

Agenda Item	Report by
1. Welcome	AB
2. Update/issues from minutes of meeting on	AB
3. New programmes:	AB
a. SC27	
b. SC28	
c. SC29	
d. Workshop for SC27 tutors and assessors	
4. Progress on SC25 programme	CD
5. Progress on SC26 programme	EF
6. Centre developments	AB
7. Feedback from EQA visit	AB
8. Update on candidate progress/update database	GH
9. IQA Reports	AB
10. AOB	ALL
11. Dates of future meetings	AB
12. CLOSE	

APPENDIX 11: EXAMPLE INTERNAL QUALITY ASSURANCE REPORT 1

Internal Quality Assurance report

IQA: Assessor: Qualification: 6312-43

Learner Name	LO/AC Sampled	Evidence Sampled	Comments	Actions to be taken by Assessor	Response from Assessor

IQA Signature _____   Date _____

Assessor
Signature _____   Date _____

APPENDIX 12: EXAMPLE INTERNAL QUALITY ASSURANCE REPORT 2

This is an example of typical content that might be contained in a report resulting from an annual IQA review. The following example has been produced by an IQA. It contains mainly quantitative data.

IQA Name _____   Date _____

Period _____ to ___ _____   Team _____

Centre _____   Centre No _____

- The Lead IQA completes the annual review of how each qualification route performs to inform the Self-Assessment Plan for the centre. The purpose of the review is to get a clear picture of how teams are performing, to gauge any trends in qualification routes and to monitor how learners are progressing.
- The review is never totally accurate as the **findings are based solely on what is recorded in the learner files on the e-portfolio Learning Assistant**. This is one of the reasons why it is so important that all team members keep accurate, detailed and up-to-date records at all times. If these are not fully complete then the figures will not be a fair representation of each assessor's work or the learners' progress.
- Attendance levels have generally remained consistently high. This is despite the fact that most assessors have increased their allocation of learners. It is also very encouraging to see that the rates of attendance at session are increasing.
- The review considered the number of completers between September 2010 and July 2011. The figures contain only learners who have been certificated in this time frame.
- The report also analyses the number of learners having additional sessions with their assessor and compared the number of session with those contained in the Individual Assessment Plan (IAP) agreed at the start of the programme.

Assessor name	Number of learners 2009	2010	Average attendance 2009	2010
A	28	42	76%	92%
B	25	31	77%	81%
C	23	0	69%	N/A

Assessor name	Learners requiring additional sessions 2009–2010	Learners requiring additional sessions 2010–2011
A	10	15
B	12	20
C	9	N/A

Assessor name	Average achievement time 2009–2010	Average achievement time 2010–2011
A	20 months	17 months
B	20 months	24 months
C	17 months	No completers

Team	% of learners retained 2009–2010	% of learners retained 2010–2011
Customer Service (including apprentices)	98%	98.5%

Gender of learners	Average completion time 2009–2010	Average completion time 2010–2011
Male	15 months	22 months
Female	17 months	22 months

A number of issues have arisen during 2010–2011 that require reporting in their own right but which also illuminate the above figures:

- Both assessor A and assessor B have increased their caseload of learners.
- Assessor B took over one cohort from a previous team member and has taken remedial action to support them to achieve. They had previously not been progressing as anticipated.
- Assessor C is no longer working with learners on this qualification.
- There has been an increase in the numbers of learners needing additional support.
- Achievement rates have increased for both male and female learners in the most recent cohort as they are working on the revised version of the qualification.

Conclusions

- The first cohorts on the revised qualifications are taking longer than groups on the previous version of the qualifications.
- Learners need more support on the revised qualifications than they did on the predecessor qualifications.
- Attendance and retention figures have improved on 2009–2010.

Recommendations

- IQA to monitor workloads on a monthly basis.
- Further standardisation at the 12 month point and end of first cohort of learners on revised qualifications.
- IQA to produce interim report on progress on new qualifications.

APPENDIX 13: EXAMPLE INTERNAL QUALITY ASSURANCE REPORT 3

Some internal quality assurance reports may contain only qualitative information. These sorts of reports might arise from a range of activities or in response to a variety of needs.

The example below contains overall impressions and comments arising from a sample of a particular cohort and is aimed at the assessors working on the programme.

This summary report directly arising from a sample would be produced in addition to the feedback from the IQA to individual assessors.

1   The portfolios were very advanced – all learners are on target against their Individual Assessment Plan and are making good progress.
2   The programme structure is working extremely well – with an induction session, two workshops, one-to-one meetings, two observations and external assessment.
3   The portfolios were very easy to sample as all contained only relevant documents and information.
4   The learners clearly understand what they are doing and are able to record their activities in sufficient detail. Some of the answers to the written questions were of a particularly high standard. Throughout all portfolios learners demonstrated good levels of understanding.
5   The learners seem to have readily accepted and implemented feedback from their assessors.
6   The observations carried out by all the assessors were detailed and thorough. Subsequently the observations carried out by the learners were also of a very high quality – detailed and precise.
7   The use of external assessors to carry out the second observation seems to be working very well.
8   During the IQA interview of learner L Trent the learner commented that the assessors were flexible in their approach and that he had been supported in what he was doing. He also said that the programme was well structured – he knew what he had to do by the end of each month and he found the Learner Plan useful to help him remember what action he needed to take between meetings with his assessor.
9   The learner records on the e-portfolio Learning Assistant were well maintained, consistent and complete.

APPENDIX 14: APPEALS LOG

No	Date Appeal lodged	Name of appellant	Outline of appeal	Action taken	By whom	When	Outcome	Date of resolution
1.								
2.								
3.								
4.								
5.								
6.								
7.								
8.								
9.								
10.								
11.								
12.								

APPENDIX 15: A TYPICAL CENTRE APPEALS PROCEDURE

There are a number of requirements that must be met when formulating an appeals procedure. It must:
■ have stages
■ have a log of appeals kept – usually by an IQA
■ outline by whom/when the AO will be informed of developments
■ include the role titles of those who are responsible for its implementation
■ use the lowest and most informal level of appeal before resorting to more formal and advanced stages
■ include timescales for each stage.

Many appeals procedures include a staged process something like the following:
■ Should a difference of opinion arise about an assessment or IQA decision then in the first instance, the learner will discuss it with the assessor concerned.
■ If this does not resolve the issue, the learner is not satisfied with the outcome or if it is not possible for the learner to raise it verbally with the assessor then the following will occur:

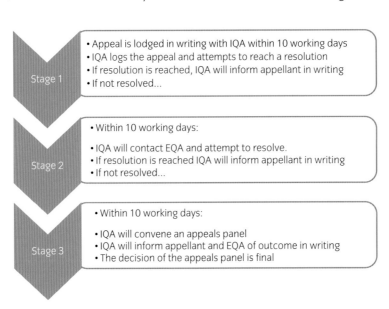

Stage 1
• Appeal is lodged in writing with IQA within 10 working days
• IQA logs the appeal and attempts to reach a resolution
• If resolution is reached, IQA will inform appellant in writing
• If not resolved…

Stage 2
• Within 10 working days:
• IQA will contact EQA and attempt to resolve.
• If resolution is reached IQA will inform appellant in writing
• If not resolved…

Stage 3
• Within 10 working days:
• IQA will convene an appeals panel
• IQA will inform appellant and EQA of outcome in writing
• The decision of the appeals panel is final

APPENDIX 16: DEVELOPMENT OR CPD PLAN

Name _____   Role _____

Learning/Development/ Action needed	By whom	By when	What will be considered success/ date completed
Comments			

Signed _____

Date _____

Name _____ Role _____

Period covered _____ to _____

Date	Evidence	Event/activity	Learning outcome	Relevance to IQA role	Duration of Activity
14 January 2010 and 25 February 2010	Minutes of meeting	Attended Employer Forums on replacements to A&V Units	Learned about how a qualification is developed. Learned about other IQA methods	Particularly relevant to IQA role	4 hours
27 March 2011	Notes from course	Attended unit 404 training day about external quality assurance	Better understanding of EQA requirements – and why they are necessary	Improved practice as an IQA	6 hours
13 May 2011	Observation checklist	Observed running a staff briefing by manager and given verbal and written feedback	Internet connection failed – now aware of lack of understanding of how link worked. Must find out more....	Relevant to many roles – all those requiring presenting and in particular use of the internet in events	1 hour 30 mins

APPENDIX 18: TYPICAL EQA DEVELOPMENT OR CPD RECORD/LOG

Continuing Professional Development (CPD) Log

Name _____   Dates from _____

To _____

Indicate in the following log the events/activities you have completed that are relevant to your External Quality Assurance role and continuing professional development (CPD). The proof that you have completed the activity should be stored in your CPD folder.

Date	EVIDENCE	Event/activity – what you did	Learning outcome – what you learnt	Relevance to EQA role	Duration
12/07/11	Notes, attendance record	Attended event about delivering 6317	Assessment strategy requirements Content of qualifications Changes to internal verification Changes needed in centres	Need to know to continue to EQA the 6317 quals Relevant to all EQA practice	6 hours

APPENDIX 19: NOS STANDARD 11 – INTERNALLY MONITOR AND MAINTAIN THE QUALITY OF ASSESSMENT

WHAT THIS STANDARD IS ABOUT

This standard is about monitoring assessment processes and decisions within an organisation, and helping to maintain and improve the quality of assessment.

TERMINOLOGY

Within this standard the following explanations and examples apply.

Assessment method	For example, observation, questioning, checking products of work, setting assignments
Candidate	The learner being assessed
Equality	A state of fair treatment that is the right of all people regardless of differences in culture, ability, gender, race, religion, wealth, sexual orientation, or any other group characteristic
Diversity	Acknowledging that each individual is unique, and recognising our individual differences in culture, ability, gender, race, religion, wealth, sexual orientation, or any other individual characteristic
Organisation	For example, an AO, internal department or any other organisation involved in assessment
Reliable	Consistently achieves the same results with the same (or similar) group of learners
Requirements for their role	This could include holding an assessor qualification and/or being expert in the subject being assessed
Sufficient	Enough evidence as specified in Evidence Requirements or Assessment Strategy
Valid	Relevant to the criteria against which the candidate is being assessed

Performance criteria

Learning and development practitioners:

11.1

Plan and prepare monitoring activities according to the requirements of own role

11.2

Determine whether assessment processes and systems meet and operate according to quality requirements

11.3

Check that assessors meet the requirements for their role

11.4

Check that assessments are planned, prepared for and carried out according to agreed procedures

11.5

Check that assessment methods are safe, fair, valid and reliable

11.6

Check that assessment decisions are made using specified criteria

11.7

Compare assessor decisions to ensure they are consistent

11.8

Provide assessors with feedback, advice and support to help them maintain and improve their assessment practice

11.9

Work with others to ensure the standardisation of assessment practice and outcomes

Knowledge and understanding

Learning and development practitioners know and understand:

KU1

The current quality requirements for assessment processes and systems in their area of responsibility

KU2

The key concepts and principles of quality assurance

KU3

The key concepts and principles of assessment

KU4

The role of the assessor and the relevant requirements of the role

KU5

The roles of those involved in maintaining the quality of assessment and the relevant requirements of these roles

KU6

The agreed procedures for planning, preparing for and carrying out assessments

KU7

Techniques for sampling evidence of assessment, including making appropriate use of technology

KU8

Appropriate criteria for judging the quality of the assessment process

KU9

How to ensure the health and safety of the learner is maintained during assessment

11.10

Follow agreed procedures when there are significant concerns about the quality of assessment

11.11

Follow agreed procedures for the recording, storing, reporting and confidentiality of information

KU10

The uses, benefits and drawbacks of different assessment methods

KU11

The types of feedback, support and advice that assessors need and how to meet these needs

KU12

Issues related to equality, diversity and if relevant, bilingualism, that may affect assessment and quality assurance, and how to address these

KU13

Procedures to follow when there are concerns about the quality of assessment: when and how to use them

KU14

Standardisation processes and how to co-ordinate and contribute to these

KU15

The procedures to follow when there are disputes concerning assessment and quality assurance

KU16

Procedures to follow when planning and preparing for, carrying out and recording monitoring activity

KU17

The requirements for information management, data protection and confidentiality in relation to assessment and quality assurance

KU18

The value and purpose of continuing professional development for assessment and quality assurance practitioners

APPENDIX 20: NOS STANDARD 12 – EXTERNALLY MONITOR AND MAINTAIN THE QUALITY OF ASSESSMENT

WHAT THIS STANDARD IS ABOUT

This standard is about monitoring assessment processes and decisions from outside an organisation, and helping to maintain and improve relevant quality assurance systems.

TERMINOLOGY

Assessment method	Ways of measuring learning and development, for example, observation, questioning, checking products of work, setting assignments
Equality	A state of fair treatment that is the right of all people regardless of differences in, for example, culture, ability, gender, race, religion, wealth, sexual orientation, or any other group characteristic
Diversity	Acknowledging that each individual is unique, and recognising our individual differences in, for example, culture, ability, gender, race, religion, wealth, sexual orientation, or any other individual characteristic
Staff competence	This could include holding an assessor qualification and/or being expert in the subject being assessed

Externally monitor and maintain the quality of assessment

Performance criteria

Learning and development practitioners:

12.1

Plan, communicate and establish procedures for the external monitoring of quality assurance systems as required

12.2

Check that internal quality assurance systems and administrative arrangements meet current requirements

12.3

Check that staffing and staff competence, assessment arrangements, methods and decisions meet requirements

12.4

Provide advice and support to help improve internal quality assurance and assessment arrangements and practices

12.5

Work with others to ensure the standardisation of assessment practice and outcomes

12.6

Follow the agreed procedures when internal quality assurance and assessment arrangements and practices do not meet requirements

12.7

Follow agreed procedures for the recording, storing, reporting and confidentiality of information

Knowledge and understanding

Learning and development practitioners know and understand:

KU1

The key concepts and principles of assessment

KU2

The key concepts and principles of quality assurance

KU3

The role of the assessor and internal quality assurance staff and the current relevant requirements to undertake these roles

KU4

The current requirements that must be met for internal and external quality assurance

KU5

The current requirements that must be met for internal assessment arrangements and practices

KU6

How to monitor and evaluate internal quality assurance arrangements and practices, including the use of technology

KU7

How to monitor and evaluate internal assessment arrangements and practices, including the use of technology

KU8

The procedures to follow when internal quality assurance and assessment arrangements do not meet requirements

KU9

The types of support and advice that organisations need on internal quality assurance and assessment arrangements and practices

KU10

The importance of providing consistent support and advice that follows agreed guidance and requirements

KU11

How to adapt monitoring and evaluation approaches in relation to customer need without compromising standard

KU12

Issues related to equality, diversity and if relevant, bilingualism, that may affect assessment and quality assurance and how to address these

KU13

Different methods of providing appropriate support and advice in line with own organisation's guidance

KU14

Record keeping procedures relating to external quality assurance

KU15

The requirements for information management relating to external quality assurance

KU16

The requirements for data protection and confidentiality in relation to external quality assurance

KU17

The value and purpose of continuing professional development for assessment and quality assurance practitioners

APPENDIX 21: ANSWERS TO ACTIVITIES
PART 2 – INTERNAL QUALITY ASSURANCE

Answer to **Activity** on page 37:
- you would need to bite one biscuit from both batches produced by each baker, ie one (biscuit) x 2 (batches) x 5 (bakers) = 10
- therefore you would bite 10 biscuits rather than 500 biscuits
- increasing the **quantity** would not enhance the **quality** of your check as they would be from the same batch and the same baker.

Answers to **Activity** on page 38:
- **interim sampling takes place** while the learner or programme is still in progress
- **vertical sampling is where the IQA samples** one unit or learning outcome across tutors, assessors, learners, sites, etc
- **horizontal sampling is where the IQA samples** something from all units or learning outcomes over a period of time
- **theme-based sampling is where the IQA samples** a type of activity across learners, eg observations or reflective accounts, etc
- **summative sampling takes place** towards or at the end of the process – usually just before certification or external quality assurance.

Answer to **Activity** on page 47:
The learners are listed, the assessor is identified – so the C and A of CAMERA have both been listed on the plan, but the following have not:
- **M**ethod of assessment
- **E**vidence
- **R**ecords
- **A**ssessment locations

This may be because they are recorded elsewhere – or it might be that the IQA has not identified which of them that she will sample at all... If this is the case then CAMERA is not being met and the sample is incomplete – and may prove to be unrepresentative.

Answer to **Activity** on page 51:
The IQA has planned an early sample of candidate Charlotte Williams and carried this out on 28.03.11 and then she has sampled her portfolio along with the others in June. She has done this because her risk assessment has raised the issue that Charlotte's night work may mean that she has less access to assessment and therefore her progress may be slower than other learners on the same programme. There may be many reasons why

some learners are disadvantaged and access to assessment is definitely one of them. In many cases working shifts – and particularly night shifts – can mean that learners struggle to make progress on qualifications because of their lack of access to and support from others – including their assessors.

The methods of assessment being sampled are not explicitly stated; however, the types of evidence imply what methods are going to be part of the sample and have been carried out.

The plan could explicitly state the methods of assessment that will be sampled and include a projected end of programme date.

Answer to **Activity** on page 61:
Whatever words you used, the culture of the centre is set by the people, their values and the actions they take inside the centre. It is important to recognise that both centres may be meeting the requirements but the first centre may be demonstrating best practice.

Possible responses to **Activity** on page 106:

1 *Your assessment records are rubbish. They don't contain nearly enough detail. Even the 'who, what, where and when' are missing.*

This is an example of how this information could be transmitted in a more positive, diplomatic and yet assertive way:

The assessment records are incomplete and so do not currently meet the requirements. They need to contain more detail and in particular accurately record who was involved in the assessment, what exactly took place, where and when it occurred, the outcome and what happens next. If your assessors record this information every time then the records will better represent what has taken place. You can find more information about good-quality assessment recording in 74. Your assessors would probably find it useful to work through the requirements of the qualification together – maybe as part of a standardisation activity. How soon could you feasibly do this? Once the records meet the requirements – if everything else is still being maintained – I would then be able to recommend that your centre be given Direct Claims Status.

2 *I don't think this person should be on the team. They haven't been an IQA for years and their CPD is out of date.*

This is an example of how this information could be transmitted in a more positive, diplomatic and yet assertive way:

The assessment guidance for the qualification outlines what an IQA has to hold and carry out in order to be able to fulfill the role. It says that the IQA has to remain active and keep their CPD up to date. This person does not currently meet either of the requirements so cannot act as an IQA until they have been brought up to date. You will need to draw up a development plan with them, with actions and target dates agreed. When they have completed the actions they will then be able to re-join the team. For example the plan could state that they will shadow an experienced IQA, carry out some joint IQA planning and attend the 'Improving your IQA practice' course that is on at the Local Office next month. It might be useful for you to send the plan through to me and I will review it for you – I might also be able to suggest a few other activities they could do.

3   *Your team has not got a clue what is required on this qualification.*

This is an example of how this information could be transmitted in a more positive, diplomatic and yet assertive way:

Before the programme goes any further you need to spend time with the team making sure that everyone understands the requirements of delivering this qualification. It would be good to get them together and go through the requirements in detail. This will enable you to clarify what they should be doing, what other team members will do and what the learners should be doing so everyone will be clear about their own role and what to expect from everyone else. How soon do you think you can do that? If it helps I can look over what you plan to do and perhaps suggest other things you might consider. As an alternative you might want to ask the AO for an advisory visit so that I or another suitable EQA can take your whole team through the requirements, discuss how they can be met and answer any queries. You need to speak to XXX at the Office or I can call them and explain if you want. You may have to pay for this visit – the Local Office will confirm this with you.

It makes sense to delay the next part of the programme until the team are fully conversant and confident with what they are doing. I will review their progress at the next visit but at the moment I can't recommend Direct Claims Status. When you have brought everyone up to speed you could request an additional EQA visit. At that point I would be able to look at what you have done and we could agree when you should re-commence the programme. As with the advisory visit you would need to request the additional visit from the Local Office and you might be charged for it – but it would speed things up.

Answers to **Activity** on page 122:

- **interim sampling takes place** while the learner or programme is still in progress
- **vertical sampling is where the EQA samples** one unit or learning outcome across tutors, assessors, learners, sites, etc
- **horizontal sampling is where the EQA samples** something from all units or learning outcomes over a period of time
- **theme-based sampling is where the EQA samples** a type of activity across learners, eg observations or reflective accounts, etc
- **summative sampling takes place** towards or at the end of the process – usually just before or even after certification.

Answer to **Activity** on page 171:

Clearly there are a number of differences between Statements One and Two and Statements Three and Four.

In Statements Two and Four the content:

- is positive about what must be done
- gives direction about where changes need to be made
- provides guidance about where useful information can be found.

However, another difference is that Statements One and Two are in the first person. They are subjective and they sound as if it is the EQA personally who has decided what the requirements are and that the centre has to satisfy the EQA.

Answer to **Activity** on page 180:

The answer is that almost all of the policies that AOs have in place relate to the EQA role. If there is a policy that requires action from a centre then the EQA needs to know about it. If it is a procedure for how the AO is going to change its own working practices – then the EQA needs to know about it. Just about everything that the AO has in place or changes has an impact on EQA practice.

INDEX